THE WORLD'S FIRST COMPUTER PROGRAMMER

'If you can't give me poetry, can't you give me poetical science?'

Ada Lovelace

THE WORLD'S FIRST COMPUTER PROGRAMMER

THE EXTRAORDINARY LIFE OF ADA LOVELACE

BEVERLEY ADAMS

PEN & SWORD
HISTORY

AN IMPRINT OF PEN & SWORD BOOKS LTD.
YORKSHIRE - PHILADELPHIA

First published in Great Britain in 2023 by
PEN AND SWORD HISTORY
An imprint of
Pen & Sword Books Ltd
Yorkshire – Philadelphia

ISBN 978 1 39908 250 1

Typeset in Times New Roman 12/16 by
SJmagic DESIGN SERVICES, India.
Printed and bound in the UK by CPI Group (UK) Ltd.

Pen & Sword Books Limited incorporates the imprints of Atlas, Archaeology,
Aviation, Discovery, Family History, Fiction, History, Maritime, Military, Military
Classics, Politics, Select, Transport, True Crime, Air World, Frontline Publishing,
Leo Cooper, Remember When, Seaforth Publishing, The Praetorian Press,
Wharncliffe Local History, Wharncliffe Transport, Wharncliffe True Crime and
White Owl.

For a complete list of Pen & Sword titles please contact
PEN & SWORD BOOKS LIMITED
47 Church Street, Barnsley, South Yorkshire, S70 2AS, England
E-mail: enquiries@pen-and-sword.co.uk
Website: www.pen-and-sword.co.uk

Or
PEN AND SWORD BOOKS
1950 Lawrence Rd, Havertown, PA 19083, USA
E-mail: Uspen-and-sword@casematepublishers.com
Website: www.penandswordbooks.com

Contents

Acknowledgements

Writing and researching a book in the midst of a pandemic was never going to be an easy task and I never imagined I would write and publish one book during that time, let alone two. So now the second one is here, it feels all the more satisfying.

Just like my previous work, *The Rebel Suffragette: The Life of Edith Rigby*, it was important that the focus should fall on a woman who managed to achieve extraordinary things in her lifetime but whom perhaps time has forgotten, and Ada fitted this profile perfectly.

As always, my thanks go to my wonderful publisher Pen & Sword, and in particular Jonathan Wright, for giving me the opportunity to tell Ada's story, to my editor Laura Hirst for her endless support and patience, and to Rosie Croft and Rebecca Lawther, whose talented social media skills come in once the book has been published, so I would like to thank them both for their past work and any future work they may do on my behalf. My thanks also to copy-editor Cecily Blench for her hard work during the editing process.

Grateful thanks go to the Society of Authors for awarding me their Authorship Grant in 2021. Writing a book during a pandemic was always going to be a huge challenge, but this money meant that I was able to dedicate more time to the writing of this book and undertake research trips that otherwise might have remained out of my reach. Their support was essential to my writing journey and has enabled me to further my career.

To my family, Mum and Dad, Chris, Paul, Alison, Mary, Danielle and my own personal champion Faith. To my wonderful friends, Emma Powell, Lorraine Mawdsley, Kathryn Baxendale, Marie Drelincourt, Gill Parker, Carol Worster, Pat Palmer, Leona Steel and Chris Smith.

Many thanks to the wonderful online support from the bookish Twitter community, for answering my endless questions, offering support and reassurance and just being a wonderful group of friends.

Finally, the biggest thanks must go to Ada herself for being such an inspirational woman with such a colourful life that rivals her father's. She has been a fascinating person to live with over the past couple of years. My admiration for Lord Byron is no secret to those who know me and I have thoroughly enjoyed getting to know his daughter. I hope I have done her life and her amazing achievements justice.

Preface

When I was trying to come up with a subject for my second book, it seemed natural that I would look for a strong, influential woman who had achieved great things in her lifetime, but whom time had since forgotten. I debated many subjects but, in the end, I decided that woman was going to be Ada, Countess of Lovelace. I came across Ada's story by default as I must confess that it was her father, the poet Lord Byron, that initially drew me to her, and I openly admit to not knowing anything of her or how influential she had been in the field of mathematics and computer science. I also must admit that even after studying Ada and her now famous *Note G*, I still have very little understanding of Bernoulli numbers and finite differences; anyone who can read mathematical equations and understand what is being said is a genius!

I have longed admired Lord Byron's poetry and I make no secret of the fact that he was the initial driving force behind this book. I have been fascinated by the man himself since my student years and one day I would love to write a book on his life, but as I like to champion the lives of women, that idea was quickly put aside for a later date and instead his daughter became a figure of interest. Writing about Ada seemed a great opportunity to combine my love of Lord Byron and my passion for bringing the lives of great women to life through my writing and, once I began to delve into Ada's life, not only was I surprised that her colourful life could rival her father's, but I was shocked at what she had managed to achieve in the field of mathematics and computer science. Computer science seems a strange subject for a Victorian, even more so for a Victorian woman, considering the lack of available opportunities for them to study these subjects, let alone be recognised for their work in those fields.

Luckily for Ada, her mother was passionate about science and mathematics, and she made sure her daughter was well-educated in those subjects, which gave Ada a solid base from which to start; that and her mother's good connections helped to place Ada in amongst the right people at the right times. So, armed with the necessary tools, she was well equipped to challenge the mathematical world and to be considered a mathematical genius. Regardless of this, she still had to prove that she could do the number work, she still had to understand very complex mathematical equations to understand how things worked.

If you look at the portrait painted by Alfred Edward Chalon in c.1840, you see a playful young aristocratic woman who is dressed in her finery, looking to the side, holding her fan; there is nothing in that portrait to suggest that we are looking at one of the age's most influential women – she looks like what she was, the pretty wife of an earl. She doesn't seem like the kind of person who would be involved in writing algorithms or solving complex mathematical queries, so how on earth did she manage to get credited with the moniker of being the world's first computer programmer? She lived in an age that was on the very cusp of a technological revolution, a revolution that was dominated by some of the greatest scientists and engineers the world had ever seen, who just so happened to be male. Some women did manage to break through but, overall, like so many areas of life, it was male-dominated.

Sadly, Ada never saw what her work led to, as the full realisation of what she had achieved did not happen in her lifetime, but in the twentieth century, her work came into prominence, and she rightly takes her place amongst some of the world's most respected mathematicians.

There are many questions that I asked myself whilst writing about Ada and, unfortunately, I could not answer them all, but I do hope to answer many of them with this study of Ada's life. Ada's story touches on so many aspects of Victorian society: the scientific advancements, the role of women both as a wife and mother, and the role of being a daughter to a well-known father and a mother who devoted her life to the moral stability of her child and all the trials and tribulations that these roles brought. Ada's life was full of success but also of loss, sadness and grief. The grief at the loss of her father at the age of eight years old affected her whole life, the ill health she suffered as a youngster that ailed her body, but never her mind, her loveless yet respectful marriage and her own pain-ravaged death at a young age all add to the complex character of Ada Lovelace.

Yes, she was wealthy, but her childhood was difficult, and she was often considered flighty and unpredictable, leaving her mother with a need to keep a close eye on her. Left by her father in the sole care of her mother at just four weeks old, she had to fight the stigma of her Byron name all her life. Her father, and her mother to some extent, loomed large over her and the choices she made. But whilst she often struggled to break free from the yoke of her name, her mathematical work alongside Charles Babbage gave Ada an identity of her own. Ada's legacy lives on today and she is rightly celebrated as an influential woman of science. She is no longer just known as the daughter of such and such or the wife of so and so – she is known in her own right as Ada Lovelace, the world's first computer programmer. She led an amazing life, and this is her remarkable story.

Timeline of Events

26 January 1783	Birth of Augusta Byron (later Leigh)
22 January 1788	Birth of George Gordon Byron
17 May 1792	Birth of Anne Isabella Milbanke
21 February 1805	Birth of William King
25 March 1812	Annabella and Lord Byron meet for the first time at Melbourne House, London, home of Viscount Melbourne
1812	Publication of the first cantos of *Childe Harold's Pilgrimage*
15 April 1814	Birth of Elizabeth Medora Leigh, daughter of Augusta Leigh and Lord Byron
2 January 1815	Marriage between Annabella Milbanke and Lord Byron takes place at Seaham Hall, County Durham
1815	Death of Viscount Wentworth; Milbanke family change their surname to Noel as part of the inheritance conditions
10 December 1815	Birth of Augusta Ada Byron
January 1816	Lady Byron leaves her husband, taking their daughter with her
April 1816	Lord Byron departs England, never to return
19 April 1824	Lord Byron dies in Missolonghi during the Greek War of Independence
1826–1828	Lady Byron and Ada take a tour of the Continent
From May 1829	Ada contracts a measles-like illness which marks the start of a three-year spell of ill health

1833	Ada attempts to elope with her tutor
5 June 1833	Ada and Lady Byron visit Charles Babbage at his home to see the Difference Engine
1834	Ada starts taking mathematics lessons with Mary Somerville and attends various lectures
February 1835	Ada suffers a mental breakdown
8 July 1835	Marriage between Ada and Lord William King takes places at Fordhook, Ealing
12 May 1836	Birth of Byron Noel King, Lord Ockham
22 September 1837	Birth of Anne Isabella King
30 June 1838	Lord William King is created 1st Earl of Lovelace
2 July 1839	Birth of Ralph Gordon Noel King
June 1840	Ada begins her studies of mathematics with Augustus de Morgan
August 1840	Charles Babbage travels to Turin, Italy to present his ideas for the Analytical Engine
Late 1841	Ada suffers a further mental breakdown
October 1842	Luigi Menabrea publishes his notes on the Analytical Engine
August 1843	Ada's translation of Menabrea's notes is published; these notes included her own notes and is signed AAL
January 1844	Ada suffers a further breakdown
November 1844	Ada meets John Crosse at Fyne Court, Somerset
November 1844	Ada enters discussions to become Prince Albert's scientific adviser
28 August 1849	Death of Elizabeth Medora Leigh, Aveyron, France
August 1849	Byron, Viscount Ockham goes to sea for three years
Autumn 1850	Ada and William undertake a visit to her ancestral home, Newstead Abbey, Nottinghamshire

January 1851–1852	Ada leads a gambling syndicate and suffers heavy losses
June 1851	Ada is diagnosed by her doctors with uterine cancer
12 October 1851	Death of Augusta Leigh, London
27 November 1852	Death of Ada at 6 Great Cumberland Place, London
December 1852	Ada is buried alongside her father at St Mary Magdalene Church, Hucknall, Nottinghamshire
16 May 1860	Death of Lady Byron, St George's Terrace, Primrose Hill, London
1 September 1862	Death of Byron, Viscount Ockham, Wimbledon
Mid-1869	Ralph King (name changed to Wentworth upon inheritance) marries Fanny Heriot and Anne King-Noel marries Wilfrid Scawen Blunt
18 October 1871	Death of Charles Babbage at the age of 79
29 December 1893	Death of William, Earl of Lovelace; his son Ralph Wentworth becomes the next Earl of Lovelace1906 Death of Ralph, Earl of Lovelace, Ockham Park, Surrey
15 December 1917	Death of Lady Anne Blunt, Viscountess Wentworth

Introduction

Whilst this is a book about the life of Ada Lovelace and her achievements within the world of science and mathematics, it would be remiss of me to not delve into her parentage. In order for us to understand Ada, to know the person she was, we must fully appreciate where she came from. We cannot have a discussion about Ada without acknowledging the fact that her father was the romantic poet Lord Byron, and we cannot ignore the facts that surrounded his life and his ill-fated marriage to Ada's mother, Annabella Milbanke.

Ada's childhood was unorthodox, even for a child of wealthy parents – she lived a life of restriction, she had very little freedom and seldom left the gaze of her family. Her every move was scrutinised and discussed. So much of what happened during this time was to shape the woman she would become. Her childhood defined so many aspects of her life including her decision-making and how she approached various milestones such as marriage and motherhood. Being the only legitimate daughter of one of England's most controversial and talked about figures ensured the life of Augusta Ada Byron was never going to be a conventional one; she was always destined to live a life of drama and intrigue as many of her forebears had done, but perhaps not many would have believed she would go on to achieve such accolades in the fields of science and mathematics.

On the paternal side of the family were the Byrons, Barons of Rochdale, Lancashire, a title which they inherited in 1643 when John Byron was created the first lord. Prior to the creation of the barony, the Byrons held various positions among the English noble ranks with earlier members of the family being knighted, including Sir Nicholas Byron (1416–1503) who was assigned to the very prestigious role of Knight of the Bath by Arthur, Prince of Wales to celebrate the occasion of his marriage to Catherine of Aragon on 14 November 1501. Sadly, Arthur died not long after his wedding and Catherine went on to become Queen when she became the wife of his younger brother, King Henry VIII. It was a tumultuous time in England in the mid-sixteenth century; religion was disputed up and down the land and, thanks to Thomas Cromwell, chief minister to the king, many abbeys and monasteries were sacked and ruined, their wealth plundered during the dissolution of the monasteries. Many noble families benefited from this, as the crown was now able to sell off the buildings, and the Byrons were one such family when the king granted Sir John Byron (1488–1567) Newstead Abbey in Nottinghamshire in May 1560. The grand ruin of Newstead Abbey would later provide an ideal gothic backdrop to a family history which would cause dismay and intrigue; the goings on behind those walls would shock society for generations to come.

As time went on, the family's fortunes grew and it would be another John Byron who would continue to elevate the family further up the social ladder, when during the Civil War, following the Battle of Newbury in October 1643, King Charles I created him the first Baron Byron, granting him lands in the north of England. Clearly impressed with his showing on the battlefield, he also created him the commander of the royalist troops in Lancashire and Cheshire; he would lead these men into battle throughout the Civil War, earning him great rewards. Lord John Byron was clearly a brave man but unfortunately, being a royalist, he had backed the wrong side and, following the defeat of the royalist troops and subsequent execution of the king, he was forced to flee England and head to the continent, where he died childless in Paris in August 1652 aged 52. He was succeeded by his equally valiant younger brother Richard; he had fought at the Battle of Edgehill in October 1642 and was knighted for his efforts in the same year. Subsequent barons held parliamentary positions with William, the 4th Lord Byron, achieving a prestigious post within the Royal Household. He was appointed to the role of

Gentleman of the Bedchamber to Prince George of Denmark, husband to Queen Anne.

In terms of being a respectable family, it was all going so well; they had served their monarchs and country well and seemed to have caused no issues or been embroiled in any scandals but, as they reached the early to mid-eighteenth century, the Byrons were about to become one of the most infamous families in the country. Their fall from grace was spectacular; they went from being well-respected prominent landowners, who held coveted positions at court, to the depths of depravity in a matter of generations. All the good work which had been achieved up to this point was suddenly threatened by William, 5th Lord Byron.

Born on 5 November 1722 at Newstead Abbey, his parents were William, 4th Lord Byron, and Frances Berkeley. His father was over thirty years his mother's senior and passed away when William was only 13 years old; he inherited the title upon his father's death in 1736 but the estates were held by his mother until William came of age at 21. From a young age, he showed an interest in becoming a naval officer and, by the age of 18, he had secured the post of lieutenant aboard the flagship HMS *Victory*. Unfortunately, a life at sea was not for William and neither was a life on the battlefield. He fled from his position of captain in the Duke of Kingston's regiment during the Jacobite Rebellion, he made it as far as Aberdeen, but when battle was on the horizon, he resigned his post, earning himself the reputation of being a coward. A hero of Culloden William was not. His reasons are unclear – it may have been a family crisis, it may have been his finances but whatever the excuse, he left Scotland and returned south to England.

William grew into a handsome man. He had a love of art and enjoyed betting at the racetracks but expensive hobbies like these soon depleted the Byron coffers. He was now under pressure to ease his financial woes and it was decided the best way to remedy this was to find himself a rich bride with a dowry big enough to fill the void in the near empty Byron treasury. The lady he finally settled on was a young heiress called Elizabeth Shaw of Besthorpe in Norfolk and they were married on 28 March 1747 in London. The contrasts between the happy couple were stark. His character was flawed, he was entitled with little money to speak of, whereas she was pretty, wealthy and considered pleasant of character. Unfortunately, one trait they had in common was that neither had any sense when it came to money, and as soon as Elizabeth turned 21, her assets became the property of her husband and, before long, there were significant gaps appearing in Elizabeth's fortune. William gradually dipped into the funds. He set about making changes to Newstead Abbey, he installed a gothic folly which was large enough to hold parties, he wanted his own flotilla of gunships, and the walls were covered in expensive works of art. As time went on, William's roving eye started to become a source of embarrassment; he had long forgotten his marriage vows and embarked on numerous extramarital affairs. Despite this, the couple had four children, of whom sadly only two survived infancy to reach adulthood – a son, William, and a daughter, Caroline.

William senior showed very little interest in politics. He often neglected his responsibilities, preferring to spend his time in the country hunting rather than in London talking politics. One month after his marriage, he was appointed to the prestigious role of Grand Master of the Premier Grand Lodge of England. It was a role full of pomp and ceremony but once those trappings had subsided, he showed no inclination to actually undertake any of the duties which were attached to the role and only attended a handful of meetings; his excuse to other members was that he had been abroad, which was not always the truth. When he did finally make it to a meeting, he buckled to pressure and was eventually replaced in March 1752.

Like his father before him, William served in the Royal Household by being appointed to the role of Master of the Staghounds but, like all other posts he had held, he applied little effort to the position and was forced to relinquish the role in 1765. It appears William was the kind of man who enjoyed the glory and status that certain positions brought but, when it came to actually exerting himself to perform any task related to it, he showed a distinct lack of interest. He did not respect any position he was given – the significance of them seemed to have been lost on him, it was more what the role could do for him rather than what he could do for it. All his previous misdemeanours would pale in comparison when in 1765 he was put on trial for the murder of his neighbour and distant cousin William Chaworth. This was the lowest point any Byron had fallen and the shame it brought would stain the family's name for years to come.

The incident in question took place on 26 January 1765 at the Star and Garter tavern on Pall Mall. On that particular day, ten gentlemen convened in an upstairs room; their numbers included politicians, landowners and other gentlemen, all from Nottinghamshire, and amongst them were William, Lord Byron and William Chaworth, a distant cousin of the Byron family. The fine wine flowed fast and the conversation soon heated up when a petty dispute broke out between the two men over who had more game on their Nottinghamshire estates.

The original discussion had actually been how best to manage game on a large estate, but it soon escalated, and bets were being placed between the two as to which of them could boast most game on one acre of land. The afternoon moved on, but both men continued to snarl at each other. To the other guests, it appeared to have been forgotten and the conversation moved on; it was only when the group began to disperse that Chaworth confronted William. Fuelled by too much wine, the two men went into a dimly lit private chamber to hammer out their differences. Chaworth was a large stout man, so he definitely had a physical advantage over William, and soon they had both drawn their swords.

It is not wholly clear what actually happened in the room that afternoon, but William felt that Chaworth had aggressively lunged at him, so in a panic, he thrust his sword at him. Chaworth retaliated, landing a glancing blow on William. William then thrust his sword through his opponent's stomach. Shocked at what had happened, he rang the bell for assistance. When aid from downstairs arrived, they found Chaworth hunched over with blood pooling at his feet, with William standing by his side. Chaworth was taken from the tavern to his home; he survived the evening but died the following morning. Suddenly, rumours were flying around about what had actually happened – was this about honour or had William, still feeling slighted from the earlier fall-out, challenged Chaworth to settle their differences, man to man?

With one party dead, it became irrelevant; this was considered murder and the penalty, if he was found guilty, was death. Panicked, William went into hiding, but a warrant for his arrest was issued on 13 February, forcing him to come back to London to surrender himself at the House of Lords. From there, he was taken to the Tower of London to await his trial; however, being a Lord of the Realm meant he was granted certain privileges. His suite of rooms was comfortable and he was free to walk about the grounds and receive visitors. Due to his rank, he was tried by his peers, 124 in total, at a trial held at Westminster Hall on 16 April. The case drew huge interest – tickets were sold to spectators and soldiers were needed to keep people in check. William arrived at the Hall at 10.00 am and was greeted by the jury, which was formed by a panel of nobles; it would be these men who would decide his fate.

The prosecution stated that this was a case of cold-blooded murder and William had even gloated at what he had done before calling for help. William called no witnesses for his defence and instead chose to have a statement read out which claimed Chaworth had goaded him and disrespected him – they were both as hot-headed as each other and he did nothing worse than defend himself and his honour. The evidence had been heard from both sides and the deliberations began. The lords found him not guilty of murder, but were unanimous in deciding that he was guilty of manslaughter. He had swerved the death penalty and being a member of the nobility meant he was protected from the more severe punishment for being convicted of manslaughter, being branded on the back of the hand with a hot iron. Instead, he walked away from the trial a free man, with only a small fine to pay.

William was not a popular man before his brush with the law and his trial did little to enhance his reputation. Following his trial, many stories surrounding William's life started to circulate, some true, some not so true. Myths about him include his becoming a recluse at Newstead Abbey; this cannot be further from the truth as he went away on holiday to Belgium with his wife and sister following his trial. Other rumours included the staging of orgies at Newstead Abbey, mounting the sword he used to kill Chaworth on the wall, and there were even ridiculous rumours that he had thrown his wife into the lake on the Newstead estate and then murdered her. There is no proof he did any of these things, but one thing we can be certain of is that he led a notorious life, which earned him the nickname 'The Wicked Lord'. The Byrons continued to spend lavishly and soon the debts started to mount again, which led William to look for ways to ease the financial burden. Once again, he hoped it would be a marriage that would help – his son William was due to turn 21 in October 1770 and, as his heir, he felt it was his privilege to marry him off to the wealthiest bride he could find.

Young William's birthday was going to be celebrated in the grandest fashion and much time, effort and money were spent on sprucing up Newstead Abbey. It was going to be a family affair, with William's siblings attending along with their children; however, a Byron family squabble was set to erupt on an epic scale and threatened to destroy the family. Father and son had very different visons for young William. His father was at an advanced stage in the marriage negotiations with a young lady from a very wealthy family; the problem was he had failed to get his son's thoughts on the matter and his eye had been caught by someone else.

The younger William defied his father's instructions when, on the eve of his arranged marriage to a wealthy heiress, the young man decided to elope with his sixteen-year-old cousin Juliana, daughter of John Byron, William's younger brother. For William senior, this was utter betrayal – any hope of financial safety had been destroyed, for his niece brought him nothing of value and the embarrassment of the broken engagement was scandalous. His brother John was far from happy too; his daughter had given up the opportunity to marry well and had instead married someone with an estate which was saddled with debt. Make no mistake, this was a disaster for everyone concerned. The family as a whole condemned the match, for it brought nothing of worth to them; neither brother could offer the other anything, so the marriage settlement was worthless. Desperate for money more than ever, William was left with no choice but to start selling off some of the family's land and treasures, starting with the vast collection of art which adorned the walls of Newstead Abbey.

The collection at Newstead Abbey included works by the Old Masters Rembrandt and Van Dyck, and they were sent to Christie's in London for auction, where they raised just over £3,000. Many have accused William of doing this to spite his son and to punish him for having disobeyed him and to leave him nothing, but he needed cash, and this was the only option he had; in fact, if he had not sold these items, then there would have been nothing at all to leave William. It is unfair to judge the young couple too harshly considering the actions of the older members of their family – they obviously loved each other and took the opportunity to wed. It was reckless and thoughtless but they were Byrons, what more could have been expected of them? They did not exactly have good role models when it came to responsible behaviour; both of their fathers had conducted extramarital affairs, amassed huge debts and courted scandal on a regular basis. Sadly, young William never had the opportunity to inherit the Byron title and estates as he died on 22 June 1776 at the age of 26. His son, William's grandson, died as a result of cannon fire in Corsica in 1794, meaning the inheritance would move to John and his descendants upon William's death.

John Byron, or 'Foul-Weather Jack', as he became known, due to his frequent run-ins with bad weather, was a British naval hero who rose to the elevated rank of Vice Admiral. In May 1741, he joined the HMS *Wager* on the ill-fated journey to south America. Thankfully, he was one of the few survivors following the sinking of the ship off the coast of Chile whilst on a voyage around the world. Following the sinking, the decision was made to split the survivors into two separate groups that would head out in the hope of finding aid. One went out to Rio de Janeiro whilst the other, including John, sailed up the coast in the most horrendous weather. One night, as the crew slept on a beach, one of their boats was swept from its anchor and out to sea, leaving just one boat which was now too small to carry the remaining men, so four were left behind to fend for themselves; they had later disappeared when those in the boat returned to the island. The remaining sailors were eventually sent to Santiago and stayed there until 1744, when a passage on a French ship bound for Spain became available. John finally returned home to England in the summer of 1746. His family back home in England must have feared the worst and as no news was forthcoming regarding his fate, they probably assumed he had either been taken prisoner or had perished along with the rest of the crew.

He was clearly not deterred by this experience as he was made captain of HMS *Siren* in December 1746 and he continued to serve in the navy and undertook numerous exploration trips and was later appointed the governor of Newfoundland in Canada in 1769. He became Vice Admiral of the White in 1780 and was to become an inspiration to his grandson George years later, when he would liken his hero Don Juan to his heroic grandfather. He was well-respected and his abilities to command a ship were not lost on his superiors. Whilst his brother William was doing his best to tarnish the Byron name back home in England, John was riding high on a wave of adulation at sea. The difference between the two brothers was startling. John was far from perfect, he had numerous affairs and money issues, but he did singlehandedly try to restore the reputation of his family name. Unfortunately, it would be his own son who would drag the family even deeper into the quagmire.

John was married to his cousin (their mothers were sisters) Sophia Trevanion in September 1748 and the couple had nine children, including two sons and seven daughters. His eldest son John, or 'Mad Jack' Byron, as he was known, was born in 1757 and he was to prove the Byron ability to court controversy was never too far away – he took up the mantle from his uncle William in that respect. Jack struck up a love affair with the married Amelia Osbourne, Lady Carmarthen. The lovers were caught together by her husband's servant, by which time Amelia had fallen pregnant with Jack's child. Unsurprisingly, Lord Carmarthen filed for divorce on the grounds of adultery, but he was a very amiable and generous man who granted his wife a considerable fortune. In true Byron fashion, Jack was not going to pass up an opportunity to get his hands on the money, so in June 1779, the couple were married in Mayfair. Their only surviving child, a daughter named Augusta, was born in January 1783. Sadly, a year later, Amelia died, leaving the infant Augusta in the hands of Jack. Amelia's death meant he was now free to marry again, which he did when he was in need of funds, in May 1785.

Jack became desperate to continue with his lavish lifestyle and was on the lookout for a wealthy bride, who would enable this to happen. Spurred on by rumours of her great wealth, he married Scottish heiress Catherine Gordon, the 13th Laird of Gight, a title she held in her own right. Sadly, this was not a love match, at least not on his part. Jack saw the pound signs and made his move. Things were about to come crashing down for Jack when he realised Catherine's fortune was tied into her family's Scottish estates, from which they were only awarded a modest income; had he been less reckless, he might have discovered this prior to the wedding.

In constant need of funds, Jack took his wife's surname in order to secure the title of Laird of Gight, but he quickly learnt he had no claim on this title, or his wife's money, and any demands he made for extra funds had to be met by Catherine herself. Soon enough, the couple were in financial trouble and were left with no option but to sell the ancestral home of Gight Castle to the Earl of Aberdeen and relocate back to England. Down on his luck and strapped for cash, the news came that Jack's father had died in April 1786. Jack thought he would be in for a tidy sum of inheritance, but unfortunately for him, John had bequeathed his son just £500. Disappointed and angry, Jack left his heavily pregnant wife in London to face the birth of their first child alone and set off for a better life in France.

On 22 January 1787, Catherine was safely delivered of a son, whom she named George Gordon Byron; Byron's birth was not a significant event to the wider world and passed without much comment. Catherine went into labour in the back drawing room on the first floor of a house in Holles Street and in attendance to help were a doctor, a nurse and a midwife. It was an arduous lengthy labour and when the child came, he was born with the caul still over his face. He also had a deformity that affected his foot and lower leg, which has been described as a 'club foot'; however, modern doctors still debate the exact nature of the deformity. It led to muscle wastage in his lower calf, which caused him to limp his whole life. He was made to wear specially adapted shoes that would support the foot but also, from an aesthetic point of view, were designed to look like an ordinary boot. His foot caused him great torment and discomfort his whole life; he often blamed his mother for his disability and in later life saw it as metaphor for his sinful life. George Gordon Byron was baptised on 29 February at Marylebone Parish Church. His godparents are noted as being the Duke of Gordon and Colonel Duff, both kinsmen to his mother.

In the summer of 1789, with little money, Catherine returned home to Aberdeen with her young son. Jack soon reappeared, following the birth of his son, and the couple tried once more to live as a family in Scotland, but soon enough money became an issue between them and when Jack realised there was none to be had – any spare funds

Catherine had had been used to care for their son – he decided to move on and in September 1790 he left Aberdeen and headed once again for France. Neither Catherine, nor their son, would ever see Jack again. He died penniless on 17 August 1791 in Valenciennes, France, aged just 35, leaving the 4-year-old George to pay his debts.

'Mad' Jack Byron was a man who never grasped the reality of life; he suffered from the same ailment his uncle had – entitlement. There were rumours of an incestuous affair with his younger sister Frances, and it would be her he ran to when he wanted to escape the company of his wife. He was known to dislike women and children and felt he had a right to be treated as a member of the aristocracy because he bore the Byron name and felt he should have been able to live a life of grandeur as a member of an aristocratic family, but unfortunately for him, he never had the aristocratic money to fund that kind of lifestyle. He caused an undue amount of torment to his family; he was an abominable son and an even worse husband and father, running up untold debts his own father was forced to settle on his behalf. His skills at being a husband were terrible; poor Catherine was driven to fits of temper and despair at his behaviour. He was an even worse father, and someone who was hell-bent on having a good time, regardless of the cost both in monetary terms and on his family. He appeared to have no redeeming qualities which could be attributed to him but that did not prevent his son idolising him later – he was keen to protect his father's memory, despite not remembering him in life.

William, 5th Lord Byron, drew his last breath at Newstead Abbey on 21 May 1798 at the age of 75. He had outlived his son and grandson, which meant his great nephew, a 10-year-old boy from Aberdeen called George Gordon Byron, was now 6th Baron Byron. This boy was to become Lord Byron, the poet, the lover and the most notorious of them all, which was quite an achievement considering what had gone before. It was perhaps good fortune his father was no longer alive, as he would have sold Newstead Abbey down to its bare bones, bleeding it for all the money he could.

All these people who made up the Byron family history had stories that would be passed down the generations. They lived life to the full, they were all charismatic and had the ability to draw attention to themselves, they courted scandal and lived way beyond their means. It was this Byron blood that was inherited by Ada through her father and his forebears before him. Being a Byron would play a significant role in her life, it would be the main focus of her childhood and would cause her to question her own sanity and behaviour when she was older. Would she be able to achieve the kind of greatness that would lift the family's reputation from the gutter back to greatness? Being a Byron, and not just any Byron, but Lord Byron's child, would ensure that no matter what she did, it would be questioned and scrutinised by society. Those charged with looking after Ada would have to be ever watchful of her, lest she follow her relatives down the path to ruin.

Chapter One

Lord and Lady Byron

Is thy face like thy mother's, my fair child?
Ada! Sole daughter of my house and heart?
When last I saw thy young blue eyes they smiled,
And when we parted – not as now we part,
But with hope.

Byron did not publicly write about his daughter very often, but he did speak of her openly in letters to family and friends, and he made mention of her in one of his most famous poems. The above stanza opens the third canto of Lord Byron's epic poem *Childe Harold's Pilgrimage*. This section was written and published in 1816 whilst he was travelling on the continent following his self-imposed exile from England. The opening two cantos had been published to huge acclaim on 10 March 1812, the same year he made his debut speech in the House of Lords, in which he opposed the Frame Breaking Bill. The poem sold out in just three days and in doing so it catapulted Byron into becoming an overnight superstar, a man the country became obsessed with. He wrote the first two cantos whilst travelling in Europe, mainly Greece and Turkey, and he used *Childe Harold's Pilgrimage* to convey his personal feelings surrounding the social unrest that was sweeping the continent at that time, mainly the French Revolution and his own country's relationship with France.

Byron had long had a fractious relationship with his country of birth; he often seemed at odds with it and the establishment, bitter at the treatment he had received from the people; one minute he was the darling and the next he was fleeing. Following his exile,

1

he commented in a letter to his publisher and friend John Murray in 1819:

> I'm sure my bones would not rest in an English grave, or my clay mix with the earth of that country. I would not even feed her worms if I could help it.

Childe Harold's *Pilgrimage* is a reflective piece that looks back on the fall-out from that momentous moment in French history. At the time of the revolution, Britain was seen as a defence against the social destruction across Europe, and Byron is looking back at this nearly a decade later with a degree of hindsight, but he sees that the fundamental aim of the revolution, that is to say to give power to the people, is failing.

Byron used the poem as a mouthpiece to highlight his own country's failings within the social and political arena and he does this through the eyes of a traveller. He is described as a romantic hero who has drifted from one place to another in a melancholic haze, disillusioned with what he has seen happening in the world, and then seeing those flaws reflected back into his own character. He has often displayed evil tendencies and yearned for a love that was always just beyond his reach. He has lived a life full of sin and debauchery and embarked on many illicit love affairs, slowly drifting from one doomed scenario to another, all of which have caused him to reveal tendencies to madness. Due to his wayward actions, he tries to lose himself into an abyss, but he is beyond redemption. He is a character who is constantly trying to press the self-destruct button on his illicit life – a product of his age, a romantic hero with a tortured soul, unable to turn away from badness, no matter how much he craves goodness.

This all sounds rather Byronic, and many people believed Byron modelled this character on himself. It can be seen as an autobiographical account of the poet's life abroad; he certainly had the reputation to match and had reached a point in his life when he could no longer maintain the lavish lifestyle he had lived since becoming the Baron. But it is a rather strange poem to make reference to your young child in; it is not a happy poem about a parent's love for their child and Byron is certainly not reflecting on that when he mentions Ada. She was his torture – in fact, when she was born, he even called her an implement of torture, but he is not making that comparison in terms of her as a person, rather the torture refers to what his heart has suffered at not being able to be a part of her life. The stanza indicates that perhaps Byron had once garnered a hope of meeting his daughter again, at some point after Annabella left with her. However, things moved fast for Byron and as he sailed from England in disgrace, he realised that would probably never happen. As their lives grew further and further apart, Ada was being brought up in ignorance of who her father was and why he was not a part of her childhood.

The publication of *Childe Harold's Pilgrimage* in 1812 drew a lot of attention Byron's way and, soon enough, he was living the life of luxury, but like so many of his ancestors before him, he had some serious issues with money. The estate he had inherited was debt-ridden from the start and never really yielded the rewards it was capable of and, of course, he lived beyond his means. But soon enough, his money worries would be the least of his problems, as there were also some serious concerns being raised in certain quarters over the nature of his numerous love affairs with women and men. He had to take action to relieve this situation and the only acceptable step he could take to redeem his tarnished reputation, which could not only solve the issue of money, or the lack of it, but also deflect the unwanted interest into his love affairs, was to marry.

He could not just marry anyone, and finding the right bride was essential if he was to drag himself back from the abyss his epic hero had stared into. Undoubtedly the young lady in question had to be wealthy with an unblemished character, be well-connected socially and, if at all possible, be considered a beauty. After all, this lady was going to be the person who saved Byron, and his reputation, she was going to pull him back into respectable society and ensure his image remained spotless. But Byron was a Byron in every sense of the word, and this was not going to be an easy task for any woman to take on.

Lord Byron could have had his pick of any woman, that was how he ended up with the reputation he had, but to get one who ticked all these essential requirements narrowed his options somewhat. There was one such lady who met all the criteria and she was Anne Isabella Milbanke, or Annabella, as she was known.

Born at Elemore Hall in County Durham in May 1792, Annabella Milbanke was the daughter Sir Ralph Milbanke, 6th Baronet, a provincial landowner and Whig MP from the northeast of England. Her mother was the Honourable Lady Judith Noel, eldest daughter of the 1st Viscount of Wentworth. The couple had been married for fifteen years and had given up on ever having children when Judith fell pregnant and Annabella was born; she was a longed-for daughter and, as a result, was petted and pampered throughout her childhood by all those around her. She was pretty in an ordinary kind of way but was not considered a beauty in the truest sense, and her character was vastly different to that of Byron's other conquests. His normal liaisons were with society beauties, women who were attractive and looked good on his arm but perhaps lacked the wit of conversation, but he needed to move away from that stereotype, he needed his new bride to be the exact opposite of this, and unfortunately for Annabella, she fitted the bill perfectly.

Her looks were mediocre and sadly there was not much to recommend her in terms of her character either. She was considered by many to be haughty, serious, and rather dull, she seemed to lack any notion of fun, and she was also deeply religious. Despite not being beautiful and witty, she was very intelligent; as their only child, her parents ensured she received an excellent education, so they employed a former tutor from Cambridge University to instruct her in the sciences, classical literature, and mathematics. He took his role seriously and taught her to the level of any other student at Cambridge.

Annabella was religious and deeply moral, which begs the question of how she ever came into the same sphere as Byron. She was also described as being cold, which gave her the ability to detach her emotions from any situation. It also meant she was able to read the great love poems of the day and not be drawn into their romantic ideas or be affected by the characters. Because *Childe Harold's Pilgrimage* was autobiographical, it drew many people to Byron; they wanted to meet the troubled traveller and compare him to the writer. This was especially true of women – they saw in the poem a man who needed to be tamed – but Annabella would not be one of these women. She was able to keep her emotions in check and initially resisted the Byron charm, but even she soon fell under his spell. She managed to convince herself it would be her religious and moral duty to attempt to rescue the soul of one who was as morally corrupt as him; it had nothing to do with his devilishly handsome good looks, or so she told herself.

Annabella confessed to her mother that she would never dream of approaching him herself, she was always one for adhering to society's rules, but she would certainly meet him, should he make the invitation. For Lord Byron, Annabella's biggest draw was the fact that she was set to inherit a vast fortune via her heirless uncle Lord Wentworth; he had children but none of them were born in wedlock, much to the benefit of his sister's family. Upon his death in 1815, Lady Milbanke and her cousin Lord Scarsdale jointly inherited the Wentworth estates, although neither held the title, and subsequently, when they both passed away, the estate was inherited by Annabella, at which point the title was reinstated and she became Baroness Wentworth in her own right. At the point of the inheritance, the family name was changed from Milbanke to Noel.

Annabella was well-connected in terms of society. Despite her father being only a minor baron, tucked away on the northeast coast at Seaham Hall, his younger sister, Elizabeth, had married Peniston Lamb, 1st Viscount Melbourne, and their son, William Lamb, would later become the Prime Minister under Queen Victoria. Annabella had many influential acquaintances in society and at court which, coupled with an impending inheritance, made her one of the most significant and most sought-after ladies in London society. It would be Byron's friendship with Elizabeth Lamb that would be instrumental in bringing her niece and the poet together, which in turn would spark one of the most talked about and unlikely marriages of the age, for you could get no two people so unalike in character.

They first met in March 1812, and with Byron riding high on the success of *Childe Harold's Pilgrimage*, he was the man to know and to be seen with. People clamoured to make his acquaintance and to share the same company as he; to be able to breathe the same air as Lord Byron was considered quite the thing. The level of success the poem achieved seemed to have been unexpected and he was quoted as saying, 'I awoke one morning to find myself famous.' Famous he most certainly was, but as far as Annabella was concerned, Byron was a project; he was someone she could observe from a distance. At dinners and parties, she would quietly stand back and watch him, all the while paying close attention to his mannerisms, watching how he interacted with various other people. Assessing him in a social environment and keeping her distance meant she was able to stand by and observe him without putting herself under any scrutiny – it kept her safe from his glare and from conversation.

But ultimately, regardless of her reported primness and self-control, Annabella was a woman and, like most other women in London at the time, she soon learned she could not resist the magnetic pull towards him. It is often said that Byron had such charisma and aura about him that he could draw people to him with hypnotic ease and, once they were in his company, they became under a sort of spell that many people found irresistible. He was considered incredibly handsome and utterly seductive and now, with his poetic successes, he was even more alluring. Annabella soon found herself being drawn towards him, unable to stop herself from being sucked into the Byron sphere.

Curiosity got the better of Annabella and she eventually built up the courage to introduce herself to him and, to her surprise, he had heard of her through her patronage of fellow poet Joseph Blacket. Annabella had a keen interest in poetry following her studies and, regardless of how sensible she was and knowing a little of his questionable character, for she must have heard the gossip, she could not pass up an opportunity to engage with the country's most celebrated poet of the day. During their first meeting, Byron made a good impression on Annabella, showing himself to be kind, charming, and considerate of her feelings, and with that she decided she wanted to get to know him better. She described him to her mother as a bad man but a good man; how her mother felt about her only daughter forming a friendship with someone of such a questionable character we can only imagine, but at this stage, it all seemed like an innocent encounter.

As time went on and their paths increasingly crossed at more social engagements, it soon became apparent to Annabella that her feelings for Byron were developing into something much stronger than a passing fancy into his character; she was now starting to feel pangs of emotion and the more time she spent in his company, the more she began to admire him. As far as Byron was concerned, he enjoyed her company, he thought her intelligent and engaging and joined in with her on discussions about poetry; he liked Annabella but he thought her different to other women. Despite her growing admiration and interest in him, never once did Annabella fawn over him or descend into unparalleled giggles at the thought of being in his company or talking to him. She had the ability to see past all that and appreciate him for being a well-mannered, polite, and friendly acquaintance, who she could enjoy engaging and enlivening conversations with. He just so happened to be incredibly handsome and the most famous man in the country, but Annabella was a sensible young woman who had been brought up with good manners and decorum – she was not the kind of person who would let her guard down for the sake of a man, regardless of who that man might be.

As time went on, the ice queen began to melt, and the more Byron got to know Annabella, the more he could appreciate her intelligence; with her, he was able to enjoy conversations with a woman who was clever and amiable, something he had perhaps not looked for in the fairer sex before. Annabella was the complete opposite of those women who clung to his coat tails in the hope he would notice them, and there were plenty of them knocking on his door. One such woman was Caroline Lamb and, in 1812, she and Byron conducted an illicit love affair that lasted several months.

It was a tempestuous and all-consuming affair that shocked society; it brought together two of society's most unstable and wayward people. They did much to deny their relationship but for Caroline this was a true love match, and her behaviour quickly became obsessive and could be just as extreme, if not more extreme than his, and he quickly grew bored of her constant attentions and stalker-like behaviour. There was no chase where Caroline was concerned – she was a willing lover to Byron and put up no resistance against his advances. She was a match for Byron in terms of character, she could not be shocked, both were unstable and nothing he said or did put her off. That kind of behaviour in a woman unnerved him and soon enough he was doing his best to avoid her company. Unfortunately for Byron, Caroline had developed a very unhealthy and obsessive passion for him; she would track him across London, sending him snippets of her pubic hairs in the post and, when her undying love was not reciprocated, she lost all sense of control. When Byron finally broke off the affair, she threatened to kill herself if he did not return to her. It is also widely accepted it was she who coined the now famous quote about Byron being 'mad, bad, and dangerous to know', and his persona has never managed to shake off this claim.

In an interesting turn of fate, Caroline was the daughter-in-law of Lady Melbourne, Annabella's aunt, and she was married to William, although she died before he became Prime Minister and therefore never held the title of Viscountess Melbourne. She was therefore cousin by marriage to Annabella. These family ties put Caroline in prime position to cause trouble for Byron and his potential new love interest. She offered to be the go-between for the couple and when Annabella sent Byron some lines of her own poetry for him to comment on, she saw an opportunity to take matters into her own hands and filter the responses Byron returned. Given the relationship between the two, it is surprising Byron would entrust any information to Caroline, but he did and she decided it was an ideal opportunity to cause trouble.

He had told Caroline he felt Annabella was too good for him, which to be fair she probably was, and that he had no desire to become better acquainted with the young heiress. But the disgruntled and jealous Caroline decided not to tell Annabella what Byron's true feelings were and instead left her of the opinion that he wanted to continue their correspondence. So, rather cruelly, she encouraged Annabella to keep the lines of communication open and to look for affection where there was none to be found. Caroline was devious and calculating and was clearly manipulating Annabella in the hope she would pester Byron to the point he would lose any respect he had for her. Her wicked plan was clearly one that she hoped would destroy Annabella's feelings for Byron; she hoped he would retaliate in a way that put her firmly in her place and out of his reach. Caroline was working for her own ends, blindly hoping Byron would return to her in his despair and their illicit affair could resume.

Unfortunately for Caroline, the plan backfired on her, and Annabella's emotions began to deepen for Byron. He finally decided he had had enough of his eccentric and unpredictable lover and her wayward behaviour once and for all – he wanted to be rid of her. When Caroline discovered she was to be cast aside, she was devastated; she had lost Byron for good and her outrageous behaviour embarrassed her family so much they sent her to Ireland in the hope that it would calm her down, so extreme had her antics become. Despite his insistence that their relationship was to end, he rather cruelly continued to correspond with her during her exile and, when she returned to London in 1813, she must have harboured hope their relationship would resume. He had given her false hope, which turned out to be far more damaging to Caroline than anyone could have imagined. When she returned from Ireland, Byron advised her that under no circumstances would they ever be reunited; this shattered her and this tumultuous affair finally came to a shocking conclusion during a ball held in honour of the Duke of Wellington, when Byron publicly slighted Caroline. In her despair and in a desperate last-ditch attempt to lure Byron back to her, she smashed a glass and cut open her wrists in front of the guests. Thankfully she did not cause any serious injury to herself, but society was shocked and outraged at what had happened. Not surprisingly, her mental stability was questioned, and Byron merely brushed off the incident as an act of attention seeking, but this was a further scandal that attached itself to the Byron name and dented his increasingly fragile reputation even more.

Caroline was a volatile person and remained obsessed with Byron for much of her life, but she was also someone whose life was emotionally challenging. Her marriage was initially a happy one and they produced two children, a son named George Augustus Frederik and a daughter, who died shortly after birth. Their son was born with mental difficulties and was cared for at home by his parents; the strain of this must have been very hard for Caroline to bear. She was not liked by her husband's family, and she never had a good relationship with her mother-in-law. Caroline died in January 1828, aged just 42 years old.

Following the end of his affair with Caroline, Byron turned to her arch enemy and his confidante Lady Melbourne in an attempt to move on and, in doing so, he finally confessed to her that he did in fact have feelings for Annabella. He claimed he knew little of her wealth and prospects but did find her pretty and clever despite not loving her, but in his view, love did not matter so much when choosing a wife. That is a rather sad way for a romantic poet to consider marriage, who you would think would only marry for the deepest of love and the most ardent of passion, especially when you consider the nature of Byron's personality, but by this time, he was desperate for funds and could not be too picky in his choosing. However, the point of being with Annabella was that she was the opposite of what people would have expected from him, the opposite of Caroline Lamb. He needed a cover, and she was the perfect foil to his outlandish lifestyle; the scandal with Caroline needed to be forgotten and marriage with Annabella was the ideal way for that to happen. Byron could not afford to have another scandal attached to his name. Lady Melbourne, however, was far from convinced of the poet's true feelings for her niece and saw exactly what he was hoping to achieve through this marriage. In her mind, she was convinced he was looking for a hasty marriage just to rid himself of her deranged daughter-in-law, and she was probably right, but he managed to persuade her that his feelings for Annabella were honest and true and a marriage proposal was made via Lady Melbourne, which would undoubtedly have given a weight of credence to the offer.

In true Annabella fashion, she took this proposal very seriously and gave it some thoughtful consideration. She even went as far as making a list of pros and cons, weighing the various outcomes against each other and what could be achieved should she accept the offer. To be fair, you cannot blame her for being cautious, for she was not Byron's type – she must have questioned his motives and asked herself if he did truly love her or whether there some other reason for his offer. In the end, her head and heart came to different outcomes and on this occasion, she decided to take heed of the thoughts in her head, and she declined the offer.

Annabella was the kind of young lady who would always listen to reason; rarely would she let her heart or emotions win out. Whether she took external advice or not, we do not know, but as things stood, any chance of a romantic relationship with Byron was now over. Rather than be dejected and feel slighted, he took the rejection in good spirit and resolved never to discuss the matter again and instead hoped that he and Annabella would remain on good terms and firm friends. Byron's good nature in the rejection may be a sign that he felt he had had a lucky escape, and in all honesty, he never truly wanted the match, or at least he never wanted the match in its truest sense, and certainly not in the same way Annabella would have wanted it. To him, this was not a romantic proposal, merely one of convenience, and his sense of relief was palpable. Being a poet, Byron chose to take a philosophical view of the situation; he saw himself and Annabella as two parallel lines destined never to join, he even referred to her as the 'Princess of Parallelograms' in reference to her mathematical and scientific education, which he admired so much in her. Over the coming months, their paths did cross again, but they never actually became fully reacquainted until Byron's older half-sister Augusta Leigh arrived on the scene.

Byron was now back on the market. He had managed to rid himself of Caroline and dodged marriage to Annabella; just by making the marriage proposal, he could show society that he was in fact a decent man who was looking to settle down with a nice young respectable lady, but Byron being Byron meant scandal was never too far away, especially when another Byron was added to the mix.

Augusta Leigh was Byron's older half-sister, the surviving daughter of the marriage between John 'Mad Jack' Byron and Amelia, Lady Carmarthen. Their marriage had not lasted long, and Amelia died whilst her daughter was still young, which led to her being passed into the care of her maternal grandmother, Lady Holderness, who raised her until her own death just a few years later. To Jack Byron, children were a drain on funds, so it is not a shock to discover Augusta's father showed very little interest in her, behaviour he would later repeat with his son, and she continued to be passed into the care of various relatives.

Byron and Augusta knew very little of each other during his early childhood; their paths would not have crossed, given that their father passed away when Byron was young. Their first meeting came in the spring of 1803 in London. He was 15 years old and a student at Harrow School and she was 20. Byron describes Augusta as being his nearest relation and she also provided him with a link to the father he never knew yet idolised, and he seized upon the chance to get to know her. They continued to correspond with each other, albeit rather sporadically, over the next few years, and saw each other rarely, but he valued his relationship with her and gradually over time the pair built up a friendship.

Growing up, Byron had been aware of Augusta's existence, but as they never grew up together, they were strangers to one another, which allowed a close friendship to blossom. Augusta was one of the very few people who had the ability to draw Byron's personality away from the brooding and melancholy he was so often described as suffering with to a much lighter and happier disposition. She could make him laugh and, in return, he showed her love and affection, for she saw very little of it in her marriage to Colonel George Leigh. They were first cousins and married in 1807, much to the annoyance of his family, but their marriage was not an entirely happy one. His character was questionable, he was even accused of swindling the Prince of Wales over the selling of a horse, he enjoyed town life and gambling and left her and the children for long periods of time. But despite all this, Augusta was a devoted and loyal wife and mother who did her best to protect her children when her husband lost all his money to gambling and left them destitute with nothing but his debts to pay. Byron proved to be a reliable support for Augusta and her children; he showed them love and affection, something his own childhood had lacked and helped her financially as and when the situation required.

Annabella had not seen these kinds of traits in Byron but, once she had, she decided she wanted to get to know him better and so turned to her aunt, the redoubtable Lady Melbourne, to reignite the old friendship, in the hope there might still be a flame burning somewhere deep with Byron's heart. In her impatience, waiting for

Byron to get in touch, she took a bold step and decided to write to him directly in an attempt to set his views on her right. She was anxious to tell him she too had suffered in matters of the heart, declining many a marriage proposal, and that in fact the two of them were more alike than he might imagine. Unfortunately for Annabella, her long plea was met with a rather short and blunt rebuttal; he claimed they could never be friends because if they were to be anything more, he was sure to fall in love with her and would be unable to refuse her and he did not want to damage her spotless reputation – she had proved herself to be too good for him.

A crestfallen Annabella replied rather coolly and calmly by advising him, 'I will trouble you no more.' This time, it was Annabella's turn to be on the receiving end of a refusal and, for a second time, the potential for any relationship fell flat. It is unclear why Byron chose to knock back her offer of friendship – maybe he did not want to risk the chance of marrying her. He had escaped it once and to put himself back in such a perilous situation may have unnerved him. There was also the fact that Augusta was now a more prominent fixture in his life and maybe his feelings for her were starting to cause him so much concern he felt it would be unfair to place an innocent like Annabella into what could potentially be a volatile and dangerous relationship. So, they both returned once again to their own lives, with Annabella receiving and declining numerous marriage offers, and Byron continuing to drift from one scandal to another. It would be one of these scandals that would threaten to destroy Byron and everything he was; people accepted his womanising ways, they knew him to be flirtatious and amorous, but things were about to get too near the knuckle when rumours of incest started to circulate.

People had begun to talk openly about Byron's relationship with Augusta and commenting that it was far closer than what society would deem appropriate. The pair were now raising eyebrows, as many felt it was not a normal brother/sister relationship. Taking into consideration the family's track record, especially their own father's questionable past, it was almost inevitable Augusta and Lord Byron would fall down the rabbit hole of immorality. Some might have been shocked at just how far the pair had fallen but considering they both carried the so-called bad Byron blood, did they ever really stand a chance of having a normal sibling relationship, or were they always going to be destined for terrible things?

It quickly became apparent that the relationship between Byron and his sister had developed into something that made their lives in England untenable, so they made plans to flee to Europe. So strong was their love for each other that they were willing to turn their backs on their lives in England, their families, and their friends so they could live a life together without scrutiny. But in the end, it turned out to be a step too far for both of them. They soon realised that if they followed through with the plan, it would mean certain exile and ruin, and it would seem neither was willing to risk that, neither was willing to step into that huge void and go past the point of no return.

Byron tried everything possible to divert his attentions away from his incestuous thoughts; he knew they were wrong but he couldn't help himself. Annabella had previously misled Byron into thinking she was promised to another, so he stalled in making his advance, but things were now getting desperate again, and sooner or later he would need to cover his tracks with Augusta. Around this time, he was being pursued by many women, all with hopes of securing his love, or passion at the very least, but ultimately it was Annabella he turned back to when he again offered her his hand in marriage. He may have done this somewhat reluctantly, but he knew he had reached a point of no return; he was on the brink of ruin and he needed Annabella to return him to the right side of morality, both in his own mind and in the eyes of society. She was able to provide him with a cover he could lay over his more scandalous affairs, the one with Augusta being the most scandalous of all, especially after she had given birth to a daughter named Elizabeth Medora, a daughter Byron alluded to being his own.

With all the rumours that were circulating, Byron acted quickly and made his proposal to Annabella for a second time and, unlike before, she accepted immediately. She had let him slip away once and she was not going to make that same mistake again; this time, there was no need for a list of pros and cons – she knew her answer straight away. She accepted Byron's offer and all of a sudden found herself engaged to the country's most desired man. How she must have felt, knowing that she had secured the hand of Lord Byron, we can only imagine; she quite clearly had no questions regarding his motives this time around, as she turned her attentions to her upcoming nuptials.

The first thing Annabella did was to invite him to the northeast to Seaham Hall to meet her parents. It must have been an exciting time for the family and quite a coup for such a small town to be welcoming a man of Byron's standing. The excitement was not shared by Byron himself and he was certainly in no hurry to see his bride-to-be or meet his future in-laws. It took him two months to make the journey north and he arrived two days after the agreed arrival date, much to her mother's displeasure. When he did finally arrive, relations between the betrothed couple were distinctly cool; they had not seen each other in some time and certainly the last time they had met, all talk of marriage was off the table, so this was quite a turn of events.

When he arrived, there was no passionate embrace. Instead, he took his bride's hand and kissed it rather formally. Unfortunately, his actions must have shocked her, as it caused her to make an incoherent remark and she promptly fled the room in utter embarrassment and shame, only to be coaxed back by her parents. Sadly, this first meeting could not have gone any worse. Annabella had probably played this moment over in her head for months, only for it to end in disaster, but she was understandably nervous at the meeting and needed her parents to steady the ship and soothe her growing anxiety.

For Byron, her behaviour rang instant alarm bells. This was not the Annabella he remembered from their previous meetings; he remembered her as being cool and calm and able to hold an intelligent conversation, a quality he admired in women. What he saw now was a young lady who seemed unable to hold a coherent discussion with him. It is clear she was completely overcome with nerves, which was quite a natural response, as she was meeting Byron for the first time as her future husband. Before this, she was his equal, they both held a place in society and both were intelligent, but now he was something else entirely. He had such a powerful and strong personality, it is hardly surprising she felt overcome by the moment. She was a young lady in her early twenties, on the cusp of marrying the country's most famous man, who as an aside had a very questionable character; how much of this Annabella and her parents were aware of we cannot be sure, but you would think a respectable family like theirs would not allow their only precious daughter to marry anyone who was deemed to have a dubious nature. After all, he had no money to offer her, he still owned Newstead Abbey but spent very little time there, and he could only offer her the title of Lady, so she must have assured her parents this was a love match. They never went against their daughter's wishes, so they must have been in agreement to the match.

But was there anyone on hand to warn Annabella of Byron's unpredictable nature? Perhaps Lady Melbourne could have stepped in to warn her niece, and maybe she did, but if Annabella's mind was made up, then it is doubtful anyone could have persuaded her otherwise. By this stage, she was clearly enthralled by Byron and was determined to marry him. For Byron, one of his concerns was whether she was going to be able to fulfil the role he required of her; she was supposed to be the straitlaced, respectable young woman who could rescue his tainted reputation – he did not want her to become like all the other simpering ladies who clung to him and turned to jelly in his presence. That would defeat the object of marrying her, surely the well-educated Annabella Milbanke was above that kind of behaviour. Byron was starting to feel anxious following this encounter and decided to cut short his trip and head back home to London. This was not a good omen for the betrothed couple; how on earth would she be able to marry him if she could not even hold a conversation with him in the presence of her parents in the comfortable surroundings of her own home?

Questions needed to be asked about whether the marriage would even go ahead at all following such an inauspicious meeting. He would not want to marry her if she could not fulfil the role he needed her to – it is harsh but that was Byron's motive, there was no romantic love on his part, this was purely a marriage of convenience as far as he was concerned. As we reflect back on this, it is hard not to feel some compassion for Annabella. She was far from being a silly girl who had been blinded by love; she was clever and respectable and to be treated in this manner was concerning.

Away from Seaham and Annabella, Byron could reflect on his trip. The main mistake he was guilty of in the early days of their relationship was his ability to bury his head in the sand, and so he managed to convince himself that all was well between him and Annabella, and that her behaviour was purely down to nerves. He resolved to go ahead with the marriage and hope all would be well. From her point of view, she was desperate to resolve any issues that had occurred at the disastrous meeting; a third rejected proposal would not reflect well and she quickly found the reason for her unfortunate behaviour. She had concluded that it came down to her simply not knowing how to behave in front of a man in a private setting. Whilst she had no issues in conducting herself in a social setting due to the training she would have been given, where there were strict rules to follow under the gaze of others, when it came to entertaining a gentleman in the comfort of her own home, she just went to pieces. Annabella quite clearly responded well to order and instruction but when left to her own devices, she struggled to cope.

Much to Annabella's relief, once she had explained her behaviour in her letters to Byron and he was happy with that explanation, the talk of marriage was reignited and plans were made for Byron to return north to be married. On 24 December 1814, he set off back to Seaham alongside his long-time friend and best man, John Cam

Hobhouse. Hobhouse and Byron had met as students whilst at Cambridge and had travelled extensively around Europe together. Of his friend's impending nuptials, Hobhouse claimed, 'Never was a lover less in haste.' Clearly Byron still had some major reservations about his upcoming wedding. Unsurprisingly, the pair did not make good time on their journey north and they arrived later than planned on 30 December, once again to Lady Milbanke's disapproval. She even threatened to boycott the wedding ceremony due to his tardiness but she was soon persuaded otherwise.

The couple finally exchanged vows and were married in the dining room at Seaham Hall on the morning of 2 January 1815. The ceremony was officiated by Annabella's cousin, the Reverend Thomas Noel; he was the illegitimate son of Viscount Wentworth and rector of Kirkby Mallory. Byron was a reluctant groom whilst the new Lady Byron was the blushing bride who had finally got her man. The atmosphere in the room must have been tense.

The happy couple were soon being waved off on their honeymoon, or treaclemoon, as Byron described it, by her parents to a nearby family estate in north Yorkshire, but Halnaby Hall was not to be the setting of a happy honeymoon for Lord and Lady Byron. As the carriage left Seaham, Byron clung to Hobhouse in a desperate attempt to halt the horses. The thought of being alone with Lady Byron horrified him; he was far from a happy bridegroom and quickly reverted to his sarcastic and erratic ways, whilst Lady Byron retreated to her usual quiet and reserved manner. The journey was tense and awkward to say the least, the frosty atmosphere reflecting the ice-cold January weather. By the time they arrived at their destination, it is probable both were already starting to regret the events of the past few days, and the new Lady Byron in particular must have been concerned by her husband's erratic behaviour. Byron seemed hell-bent on making this trip difficult and uncomfortable for his new wife; far from trying to put her at ease, he goaded her.

There are many accounts of what happened upon their arrival at Halnaby Hall. Some people claim Byron stormed from the carriage, leaving a distraught Lady Byron in his wake, shocked and bewildered and seriously questioning if she had made the right decision in marrying such a volatile person. But then there are some who say she was happy and laughing, just as any new bride would be. Whether this was an act she was putting on to save face, we do not know, but you could understand if she was trying to be brave; it would have been better to smile through the worry than succumb to it, for her husband would have shown no concern for her feelings. According to reports, the consummation of the marriage was far from romantic; instead, it was brusque and 'Byron had Annabella on the sofa' in the drawing room of Halnaby Hall, soon after their arrival.

The following morning, things did not improve when Lady Byron's wedding ring slipped from her finger into the grate of the fire. Was this an early omen that the Byron marriage was doomed for failure? She probably did not need that to happen to know things were not as they should have been, and things were about to get worse when a letter from Augusta arrived, causing Byron's mood to swing once more as he began to dwell on his past indiscretions. It would soon become apparent to Lady Byron that there were going to be three people in this marriage and there was nothing she could do about it; even worse for her was the realisation she was not necessarily going to be the most important woman in that relationship.

Byron's continuous rantings about his immoral past started to ring alarm bells for Lady Byron and she was soon questioning exactly what kind of relationship there was between her husband and sister-in-law. For the first time, she wondered if there was something far more sinister between the pair other than just sibling affection; if he wanted to keep this a secret from his wife then he was running the risk of her working it out. Had she married someone who was having an incestuous affair with his sister? Lady Byron's thoughts at this realisation must have been terrifying for her – her husband's actions would reflect very badly on her and her family if this was to turn out to be true. People would question whether she knew of his behaviour before they married, and if she did, then she must have condoned their actions, as she married him willingly.

Lady Byron was suddenly at great risk of having her reputation damaged beyond repair, her husband seemingly showing no regard for this; it seems incredibly reckless on his part as, considering he married her as a cover, he was close to blowing that cover wide open. If he carried on in this manner, he was at risk of being exposed as someone committing incest. Having Lady Byron as an unwanted wife would also expose his beloved Augusta to scrutiny, so it is hard to understand why he behaved like this.

Byron's dark moods and bad temper continued, and he became more melancholic as the week went on; he talked constantly of the madness that ran through his family and said that his soul was tormented and tortured. Lady Byron had no option but to sit and listen to her husband and try to make sense of his ramblings. This was far from the honeymoon she had envisaged. It appeared their marriage had been lifted straight from the pages of a gothic novel as they both plunged into the deep depths of despair; it made for a tragic start to married life for both of them. Byron felt trapped and Lady Byron's dreams shattered before her eyes. Had they both realised so early on that their marriage was a mistake, or was this just honeymoon blues? Surely Byron knew all along that this marriage was a sham, but Lady Byron seems to have been completely naïve to the fact that Byron had not really wanted to enter into matrimony but felt compelled to. She initially had her doubts about their union; coupled with the fact they had not spent a lot of time in each other's company, it is understandable that she may have felt out of her depth as a new bride; it was not a surprise that they would need a period of adjustment and time for their relationship to find its feet – that was the hope, at least.

The honeymoon week was finally over and they both left Halnaby Hall with a sigh of relief. They briefly returned to Seaham Hall to see Lady Byron's parents before they headed off to London and their married life. En route, they stopped at Six Mile Bottom near

Cambridge, which was the home of Augusta, and seeing his sister again caused Byron's mood to swing violently once more. He took up again the ranting of his dark and sinister crimes; the crimes in question included incest and sodomy. At the same time, he lost any sexual interest in Lady Byron. It is obvious his mind was elsewhere when it came to matters of the bedroom when he was in Augusta's company – he seemed to lose all sense of reason when he was in the presence of his half-sister.

If Lady Byron had any doubts over their relationship or what Byron was referring to when he mentioned his dark thoughts, she was soon going to be given a rude awakening when Byron called Medora, Augusta's young daughter, his own. He seemed to be hitting the self-destruct button again by openly admitting this to his wife; it comes across as though he was either wanting Lady Byron to disclose their secrets to the world, or he thought her so loyal that she would not breathe a word of it, lest she be drawn into his dark world. Another explanation could be that he thought so little of his wife he did not give her feelings a second thought – she was someone he could offload his secrets to without any consideration to the impact revelations like that could have on her.

He was manipulating Lady Byron for his own needs; she was his emotional punchbag and knowing she would not, or could not, turn to someone for advice meant that she had to process these thoughts by herself. She was isolated with no company other than Byron and Augusta. The news that Medora could possibly be her husband's daughter must have been the final penny to drop for Lady Byron. The realisation that her husband had been conducting an affair was bad enough, surely even Lady Byron would not have been naïve enough to think he would not have any extramarital affairs given his track record, but the fact it was incestuous with his half-sister was something else altogether.

Whether Lady Byron truly understood the full extent of what Byron meant by this statement regarding Medora's parentage, or whether she just chose to simply ignore it and pretend it was not happening, we cannot be sure. As a newlywed, she may simply have refused to believe it; his outbursts were so up and down and unpredictable that she could be forgiven for just brushing off these claims and putting them down to his normal rantings. After all, what wife would want to believe that of her new husband? The shame and embarrassment it would cause to her and her family meant turning a blind eye might have been the better option, and maybe Byron knew this would be the path she would take, hence his being free with the information.

We do know that she certainly never saw Augusta as a love rival but more of a friend and ally who could help her in understanding her temperamental and often melancholic husband. Anabella must have understood that if she was to have any sort of relationship with her husband, she needed Augusta onside. The two women enjoyed each other's company and corresponded often, so it is difficult to accept that Lady Byron was overly perturbed by their relationship; there appeared to be a genuine affection between them at this point of their friendship. It wasn't just his supposed relationship with Augusta that was a cause for concern for Lady Byron, he also alluded to being 'guilty of some heinous crime' which we can safely assume relates to his relationships with other men. Sodomy at that time in Britain was illegal and, should he be found guilty of such things, his downfall would be complete.

After the Byrons had left Augusta's home, they headed straight for London, where they set up home in one of the capital's most fashionable areas, at 13 Piccadilly Terrace, near Green Park. Now that they were established in their marital home, and away from Augusta, their relationship seemed to stabilise and surprisingly things got off to a good start. Byron's mood was lifted even further as he was happy to be back in London and amongst its society and his friends. Shortly after their arrival, Lady Byron fell pregnant with the couple's first child. Finally, all the talk of heinous crimes and madness ceased, and it seemed the marriage was on an even footing as both appeared to be happy and in love. The horrors of the honeymoon seemed to be well and truly behind them. Sadly, this was never going to last for very long.

Augusta's visits to Piccadilly Terrace became more frequent and Byron's financial worries were mounting by the day. Soon the pressure was growing. The marriage was too fragile to withstand any external crisis and it soon began to deteriorate at an alarming rate, causing Byron to once again descend into one of his dark and disturbing episodes. His moods became so unbearable that Lady Byron considered leaving him before the birth, but it was too late, and she went into labour on 9 December 1815. Augusta was in residence at the time.

Byron showed little interest in impending fatherhood or his wife's condition. He left her giving birth and went out for an evening at the theatre. Upon his return a few hours later, Lady Byron was in the full throes of an agonising labour, and Byron's behaviour took a bizarre turn when took it upon himself to start firing bottle tops at the ceiling with a poker, causing an immense amount of noise, as it was directly below the labour room. Why he did this we can only speculate – even if you had little interest in your wife or newborn child, you simply would not behave like this, unless you were perhaps jealous of the attention being lauded on someone else, but that does not seem likely. What does seem likely is that he was in a panic. His money worries had got so bad that they ran the risk of eviction; how was he going to support a child along with his lavish lifestyle? There seems to have been a lot going on in his head and any one factor could have caused this kind of behaviour. Byron seems to be very disturbed in his mind and appears to be reaching breaking point. It would not take much for him to reach the point of no return.

Despite his attempts to cause disruption, Lady Byron gave birth to a healthy baby girl in the afternoon of 10 December 1815. She was named Augusta Ada Byron, although she would grow up to be called Ada, and her father's response to her birth was mixed. He seems to have been caught in two minds about becoming a father; on the one hand, he showed little interest in her arrival, but on the other, he was concerned enough to enquire about her feet and was clearly anxious to know if she had inherited his deformity; thankfully she hadn't and she was perfect.

Upon meeting his infant daughter for the first time, he exalted, 'Oh what an implement of torture have I acquired in you!' He later commented on the infant Ada in a letter to his friend Thomas Moore. In it he claimed:

> The little girl was born on the 10th of December last; her name is Augusta Ada. She was, and is, very flourishing and fat, and reckoned very large for her days – squalls and sucks incessantly.

Byron may have been disappointed that his firstborn was a girl and not the longed-for son that men in the aristocracy wished for. If the baby had been a boy, his actions later on might have been somewhat different, as he would have been his heir; as it stood, girls could not inherit the Byron title. But a daughter it was, and she was going to have a tumultuous start to life, thanks to her father.

In the days following the birth, Byron's mood swings were back. He entered Lady Byron's rooms and raged at her, threatening to be wicked. The birth seems to have set Byron off into one of his guilt-ridden expletive rants in which he threated to return to his previous ways. He claimed never to have lived outside the law in England, but maybe had abroad. Tolerance for homosexual activity was more widely accepted in Greece and Turkey, where he would be free to express his desire and love for men without censure.

Alarm bells were ringing for Lady Byron. Concerned that he might be about to go back to his homosexual way of life and with a young baby to think about, she turned to science for guidance. She sought the opinion of Byron's doctor, the eminent physician Matthew Baillie, who was called in to observe his patient. His advice to Lady Byron was that she leave her husband straight away, taking the child with her. But this was a step she was reluctant to take at this precise moment, as she was hopeful there would be another cure available to them, so she stayed a little longer whilst alternate explanations were sought.

Lady Byron felt that in order to help her husband, she needed to delve more into the person he was, so she decided to enter his rooms without his permission to go through his private correspondence. To her horror, she found laudanum and literary works by the very controversial Marquis de Sade, whose novels were not considered fit for public circulation. She was now convinced of his insanity; the Byron madness that he so often talked of seemed to have taken hold of him. Armed with this explosive information, Lady Byron finally decided to leave her husband immediately but, before she did, she agreed with Baillie that Byron should be placed under discreet surveillance in order that his true character could be assessed.

On the morning of 15 January, Lady Byron departed Piccadilly Terrace with her four-week-old baby daughter. Passing her husband's closed door on the way out, she paused briefly, before getting into the waiting carriage and heading for her parents' home, Kirkby Mallory, in Leicestershire. Leaving Byron would not have been an easy decision for her to make, especially with her newborn baby to consider, but the time had finally come for her to admit that he had issues that went far beyond anything she could help with, and the best course of action would be to remove herself from his presence and hope the doctors could intervene and help.

We should also not underestimate what Lady Byron's actions actually meant in terms of society norms at that time. Men owned their wives and children, giving them little option but to stay, so leaving her husband was an incredibly brave move to make on her part. But it was quite clear that her life had become so unbearable that she could no longer tolerate being in the marital home. It was even more of a risk when children were involved, as the father was technically the legal owner of his children, which left the mother open to the risk of losing them, regardless of the reasons of the marital breakdown.

Surprisingly, affectionate letters were still sent between the couple, and they used loving nicknames and considerate words with each other. To Lady Byron, this was just a temporary separation whilst doctors assessed her husband's character and mind; she was clearly intending on returning to Byron and their marriage once a cure had been found for his ailments. But the doctor's results were not what she was hoping for and, much to her dismay, the only medical problem found with Byron was a liver complaint, meaning that his outbursts and depressive states were not down to any physical condition, but a moral one, and not something a cure could be found for. From this, a final decision was made, and Lady Byron decided that it would be in the best interests of both her young daughter and herself to separate from Byron permanently, using his sodomy, incest, and other immoral behaviour to justify her decision.

When the news of the separation hit the headlines, it proved to be one of the biggest scandals of the day, and it was paramount to Lady Byron and her family that she was beyond reproach and that none of her husband's behaviour affected her or her daughter in any way. After just one year, the Byron marriage was over. It was perhaps not surprising, given the distinct differences in their characters, and many would have guessed this would have been the outcome, but not many would have expected the reasons behind the split.

By the laws of the day, Byron had every right to claim Ada back from her mother, and there would have been nothing she could have done if he had come knocking on the door, demanding to take his baby daughter away. Clearly Byron was in no shape to take care of her, and if he had decided to remove her from Lady Byron's care, then the assumption would have been that she would have gone into the care of Augusta, which would have galled Lady Byron to know that not only had Augusta been a root cause of her marriage break-up but also that she was raising her daughter on behalf of Byron. Thankfully, he saw sense in the matter, and decided to allow Ada to stay in the care of her mother, although he had concerns over his mother-in-law's influence over his daughter and he was right to be, as it would be her who would prevent Ada from seeing her father's likeness.

In a letter dated 8 March 1816 to Moore, Byron had clearly given the thought some serious consideration: 'My child is very well and flourishing, I hear; but must see also. I feel no disposition to resign it to the contagion of its grandmother society, though I am unwilling to take it from its mother. It is weaned, however, and something about it must be decided.'

The fall-out from the separation and the vilification Byron received forced him out of the country. England had turned its back on its most celebrated poet and biggest celebrity of the age, leaving him with no other option but to impose exile upon himself. Byron signed the Deed of Separation and left London on 23 April 1816. The next day, he was writing to friends, begging them to pass on news of Ada; he had no desire to know the welfare of his wife, but Ada was clearly in his thoughts as he prepared to leave her behind. From London, he headed for Dover, where he set sail for the continent, never to set foot on English soil again.

Amidst the tumultuous fall-out of the Byron marriage was a baby girl who through no fault of her own had been thrust into the limelight, for she was the sole legitimate child of Lord Byron, once the hero but now most definitely the villain. This made her an object of curiosity, and she would remain so for the rest of her life. She would have to learn to grow up in the shadow of her parents' ill-fated marriage and subsequent split, and of her famous father, whose name she carried despite never knowing him. Lord Byron's figure loomed over his daughter's life like a spectre, casting a shadow on everything she did. His immoral behaviour meant that every aspect of her life would be scrutinised, not just by her mother, who was desperate to stop any aspect of her husband's persona reflecting on her daughter, but also, by society. Every decision she made meant that people would be looking to see if she would turn out like him; they wanted to know if she looked like him, spoke like him, or moved like him – how much did she resemble her father?

The fear of her inheriting the so-called Byron madness seems to have fascinated and appalled in equal measures and ensured that Ada Byron would always live her life in a way that would be watched, and people would be on the sidelines, waiting for her to make a wrong move. Lady Byron would do her very best to shield Ada from as many of the negative comments as she could and would attempt to distance her from her father's reputation.

Ultimately, Augusta Ada Byron would grow up to create a reputation all her own; it was important that she forged her own path in order to stop any comparisons with her father and, to some extent, her mother too. Her name was to become synonymous with modern-day computer science. She was a woman who revolutionised mathematic thought and one who was on the cusp of greatness in terms of what could be achieved. She embodied the Byron genius and also had that unique way of attracting attention to herself, sometimes for good and other times for bad reasons. But either way, Ada has a story of her own to tell. Independent from her parents' lives or her husband's and children's lives, she can be held up in her own right and be held accountable for all the remarkable things she achieved. Known most commonly under her married name, Ada Lovelace, she defied the social conventions of the Victorian era to become a woman who was known for her intelligence and foresight in a man's world. She may have been the daughter of Lord Byron, but Ada Lovelace was a star all of her own and this is her story.

Chapter Two

Childhood

The young daughter of Lord and Lady Byron was undoubtedly a figure of interest. With parents who were so far apart in terms of character, and having gone through a very public split, how would the young Ada grow up, given that her father had left the country and her mother was determined to wipe any trace of him from their lives? Would she notice he was not in her life, would she ask questions about who he was, where he was, and why he was not in their lives? All these questions would have to be answered by her mother at some point in time, but the biggest immediate concern for Lady Byron was that Ada might inherit her father's perceived madness and badness.

We know from the medical observations made on Byron that his behaviour was caused by his mental instability and not a physical ailment; could it be possible that this affliction had been inherited by his daughter, just in the same way he seemed to have inherited it from his father? Of course, it was likely that could happen – Byron family history proves that some form of mental vulnerability affected their ability to behave in a way that society would consider normal; this is not to say that they all suffered with this affliction, but as a parent, Lady Byron was right to be concerned and she was going to do her utmost to stop it from happening. She seemed intent, with the backing of her parents, on making Ada the complete opposite of what her father was. She wanted her to grow up to be a dull little girl who enjoyed very little social interaction with children her own age. She was to enjoy no activities that could potentially cause excitement, just in case they unsettled her mind and made her giddy.

Due to this strict regime, Ada spent much of her early childhood in the care of her grandparents, with whom she enjoyed a close relationship, at their Leicestershire home in Kirkby Mallory. Kirkby Hall formed part of a very large estate which would have provided the young Ada with copious adventures; had she been allowed to wander among its vast grounds, she would have experienced a very idyllic childhood. But it also served another important function. An estate like this ensured that Ada could enjoy a certain amount of security as it offered much protection from the prying eyes of the world outside. It also safeguarded her from any potential kidnap threat from her father. He still had the power to remove Ada from the care of her mother; even though he was living abroad, he still had the right to employ someone to act on his behalf regarding the welfare of his child.

Lady Byron and her family went to great lengths in their mission to distance Ada from her father, both physically and mentally, and that included concealing a great portrait of Lord Byron that hung in the galleries at Kirkby Mallory. The portrait in question is well-known to us today, and remains one of the most recognisable portraits that has ever been painted of the poet. It was a painting by Thomas Phillips from 1813, which depicts him in Albanian costume. It is a flamboyant depiction of Lord Byron and has been described as being a good likeness; he is aged 25 and it is said the painting shows the poet at his happiest time of life. Byron had visited Albania on his travels in 1809 and became fascinated with their dress; he sent many costumes back home to Newstead Abbey as he felt it was 'the most magnificent in the world'.

There are many versions of the painting, but the original was bought by Lady Byron's mother for 120 guineas directly from the artist and was hung above the chimney breast. There is a lot of speculation regarding this painting and its fate after the Byrons' marriage broke down. It was passed to Ada at the time of her marriage but, according to the National Portrait Gallery in London, the copy owned by the family now hangs in the UK embassy in Athens. Many state that a green velvet curtain was placed over it in a bid to stop Ada looking upon his likeness and being tainted by his immorality – she was warned never to look behind the curtain. Another, perhaps more plausible explanation for the green velvet curtain was to protect it from external damage from smoke and sunlight. But once the Byron marriage collapsed and it was clear a reconciliation was never going to happen, the portrait is said to have been removed and packed away in a box and put in the attic at Kirkby Hall, only to be reopened when Ada had reached the age of 21, and even then, it would be down to her mother to allow her to view it.

Regardless of what actually happened to the portrait during Ada's lifetime, the myth still lingers and remains bigger than its eventual fate. There does seem to be a lot of mystery surrounding this painting and if it was Lady Byron's wish that Ada was to be protected from her father and his reputation, then it does beg the question as to why the portrait would be hung on the walls in the first place, if it is to be believed that the painting remained on the wall after the split. If we assume it was, then the sensible thing to do would be to keep the portrait out of view, stored away in an attic or cellar, well away from the gaze of a young child with a curious mind. Surely it would pique Ada's curiosity even more to know that there was a mysterious picture shielded from view that she absolutely must not look at. If it is to be believed that the portrait still hung whilst Ada was a young child, then you cannot help but feel that she was being set up to fail here. Was Lady Byron goading her young daughter to be naughty? Was she testing Ada and her boundaries, for what child has the ability to not do something they are told when the prize is so alluring?

Lady Byron enjoyed having control over Ada, bending the child to her will, and making her believe what she wanted. But what were Lady Byron's true motives behind her parenting style – was there something more sinister lurking under her surface when it came to the matter of her husband? Considering her supposed hatred of Lord Byron, she did refer to him often and kept his name; surely it would have been deemed more appropriate to drop the title of Lady Byron, considering the reasons behind the split. She was so adamant about keeping Ada protected from his name that it may have been considered a prudent move to put distance between herself and that infamous name. There was also the fact that she would inherit her own title upon the death of her mother. It would appear she been lured in and absorbed by the Byron phenomena after all, as she seemed unwilling, or unable, to relinquish his name.

It is difficult to know what Lady Byron's true stance was when it came to protecting Ada; after all, she had experienced first-hand the mood changes in her husband – she had lived with him for over a year and was justified in wanting to keep Ada's knowledge of him to a minimum, and also for wanting to protect her from any possible affects it may have on her personality. Her constant protestations about Byron and his character make it look like she was trying a little too hard to convince people of her reasons for being so strict and heavy-handed towards Ada. Maybe her actions were slightly too harsh – it was almost like she was punishing her daughter; maybe she reminded her mother a little too much of her father in terms of looks. Ada was known to have shared certain physical characteristics with her father and if Lady Byron did want to forget and move on from her doomed marriage, she had a constant reminder in her daughter. But Ada was just a child; she had no concept of who Lord Byron was and what he was renowned for, so it does seem slightly unfair to expect her to endure such an oppressive childhood.

Ada was born at a time when her parents' marriage was at its lowest. The couple had endured difficult times throughout the first year of matrimony and you could be forgiven for thinking that the impending arrival of their firstborn child would bring the couple closer together, but that was never going to be, as Byron's mental state was too unstable. The fact he was about to become a father seemed to send the couple in opposite directions and so Ada was born under a cloud created mainly by him, with her mother unsure what the future held for them as a family. It was these difficult circumstances that made it difficult for Lady Byron to form any real kind of bond with her daughter. Although her motherly instincts kicked in straight away when she realised she had to remove them both from his company, as Ada got older, Lady Byron often, rather cruelly, referred to her as 'it'.

The lack of ability for connection led to the pair remaining detached for the first few years of Ada's life and she spent much of her time in the care of her grandmother, who she was devoted to, and her nurse. The lack of contact with her mother naturally had a negative impact on the young girl and unfortunately, this meant that Ada often became distressed when she was left solely in the care of her mother. She was not used to being in the company of such a domineering person and was often on edge, desperately trying not to do something that could antagonise her, which would lead to Ada being disciplined. Her behaviour was always under constant scrutiny when she was in the company of her mother, whereas when she was in the care of her nurse, she could be a freer spirit, she was a different child who was happy and playful.

Despite this, it would be unfair to accuse Lady Byron of being a bad mother. Yes, her methods were questionable, but they were understandable given the circumstances, and she took the education of her daughter extremely seriously. Deciding to educate her in the manner she did turned out to be a good move for Ada. Like her parents had done for her, Lady Byron felt it was important for Ada to have a full and enriching education; she deemed education to be a vital part of a young girl's upbringing. Whereas many girls of this time were taught the accomplishments that would help them attract a husband and enable them to run a large household when they was married, Lady Byron went beyond this for her daughter. She may have struggled to connect with Ada on an emotional level, but it was her express wish that she be tutored in intellectual and logical subjects such as mathematics and the science-based subjects; under no circumstances was she to be taught any subjects that could stir the emotions, or get her excited and awaken her Byron genes – these must be supressed at all times.

Lady Byron became almost regimented when it came to Ada's moral upbringing, and it was her wish that her daughter's self-control and character were free from self-thought and daydreaming. Her little girl was not allowed to think of all the things that other girls her age did, no thoughts of adventure or joy were permitted for Ada. In order for her education to be delivered in the way Lady Byron had intended, an army of nurses, governesses, and tutors were employed to ensure that Ada was kept out of mischief and on the straight and narrow. Sadly, none of those employed could match up to Lady Byron's exacting standards and they were quickly dismissed from their posts. It was clearly a challenge for them as well as for Ada. Lady Byron's demands in terms of the quality of lessons provided and their ability to keep Ada out of trouble were so strict it is no wonder the turnover of staff was so high; she cannot have been an easy employer to please and get along with, and the constant change of authority must have been difficult for Ada. She would have spent time getting to know and growing accustomed to new people and just when she thought she could relax and settle into her new routine, it was changed, and she had to go through the process again.

All this uncertainty meant it was an unstable atmosphere to live in and she was constantly kept on her toes in terms of those who were in charge of her welfare. It would appear that Ada was kept in a persistent state of high anxiety, not knowing when change was coming. It seems she was never allowed to form an emotional attachment to any one person, never getting enough time to get to know someone long enough to trust them or form any bonds that could provide her with an emotional outlet; all this was preventing her having the chance to love. Is this cruelty? Was keeping a young child in a constant state of anxiety wrong, or can it be justified by Lady Byron's need to protect Ada from herself? No one seemed to be too perturbed by it at the time. Lady Byron's parenting was never questioned; any outsider looking past the security of Kirkby Mallory would have seen a mother intent on protecting her child and providing her with a decent education. They would have thought Ada lucky to have such a loving and considerate mother, but there is something about the suppression and constant state of tenterhooks that does not feel comfortable from a twenty-first-century viewpoint. But as far as Ada was concerned, she knew no better. She had very few, if any, friends to converse with to know that what her mother was doing was not perhaps not the best course of action she could be taking when it came to her daughter's welfare. Of course, this is all subjective, and we look back from a place of privilege. We know of Byron's behaviour, and we know that Lady Byron's main aim was to stop any madness coming through to her daughter.

When the time came for Ada to begin her formal education at the age of five, a lady called Miss Lamont was employed by Lady Byron to take on the role of governess. She was provided with a strict curriculum that she was to teach Ada and under no circumstances was she to deviate from it. She was expected to follow it to the letter, with no exceptions, or she would be instantly dismissed. But by that age, Ada had become a persuasive little girl, and when the weather was nice, she had a knack for persuading Miss Lamont to stop the lesson to go outside and play in the gardens. How this went down with Lady Byron we can only guess. But happily, Ada appeared to thrive under the tutelage of her new governess and, according to Miss Lamont's notes, the young Ada was well accomplished at adding up, geometry, and reading, her mathematical promise already showing through.

Under Lady Byron's strict rules, each lesson was to last no more than fifteen minutes, and Ada was to be watched at all times for any signs of naughtiness. But things were not all bad and good behaviour was rewarded by the issuing of tickets. Good behaviour was deemed as being polite and obedient and having the ability to sit still and concentrate in her classes. Unfortunately, this was a task that Ada struggled with more than most, as she was an active and inquisitive child. The opposite of the ticketing system was the punishment for bad behaviour which was often doled out in the form of being ordered to stand in the corner for a length of time. On one occasion, in her upset and frustration, she bit a chunk out of the dado rail, which only resulted in causing her further distress. This was a rather alarming fit of passion that Lady Byron simply refused to tolerate, but Ada was a spirited little girl who liked to dash about here and there; she was energetic and lively, so the daily battle to be good was hard.

She does not come across as a naughty child, just an active one who did not have the ability to control her natural need to explore and when she fidgeted, which she often did, as a form of punishment, she had her hands tied into a black cotton bag. Ada hated to disappoint her mother and would cry and get upset when she thought she had let her down, but to Lady Byron, it was Miss Lamont who had let her down. After just one year in the role, she was dismissed from her post. She must have deviated from the plan once too often. It was quite clear that Ada was a young girl who was difficult to command, which could be said of any six-year-old child, but as far as her behaviour went, it was not what Lady Byron expected or was willing to put up with. Ada comes across as a normal child who is interested in the world around her, wanting to explore her surroundings, but to her mother, this was too spirited and that had to be curbed as quickly as possible. In order to try to instil some discipline into her, further punishments were devised. These new sanctions included strapping Ada to a wooden board in a bid to keep her still, locking her in a separate room, or putting her in the corner, which she took a particular dislike to, and she bit further holes in the wall.

Whilst Ada was living within her mother's strict upbringing, unbeknownst to her, her father had continued to reach out to friends for news of her welfare since leaving England. He sent her small gifts via Augusta including a small granite ball that she could roll along the floor as a toddler and a beautiful crystal necklace that she could wear when she was older. He even sent her a lock of his hair. Thought and consideration had gone into each of these gifts and show that Ada was never too far from his thoughts. Byron may not have had custody of Ada, but he still had the power to prevent Lady Byron from doing as she pleased when it came to their daughter. She had wanted to take Ada on a tour of the continent, but Byron expressly denied this request.

He instructed his friend Hanson to make sure that proper steps were in place to prevent his daughter from being removed from the country and brought abroad; he had no issues with Lady Byron travelling but under no circumstances was she to take Ada with her. Why he was so adamant about this is not clear – maybe he felt a trip like that was too much for a young girl at that age, or that the morals on the continent were questionable and he did not relish the idea of her becoming aware of certain things. He probably did not relish the chance of bumping into Lady Byron either, and as Ada's father, his word stood.

Byron's interest in Ada never wavered and he wrote to Augusta in October 1822, requesting yet more news of her. He wanted to build up an idea of the kind of person his young daughter was becoming and to know whether she was showing any signs of becoming like him:

> Your three letters on the subject of Ada's indisposition have made me very anxious to hear further of her amelioration. I have been subject to the same complaint but not at so early an age nor in so great a degree … I wish you would obtain from Lady B some account of Ada's disposition, habits, studies, moral tendencies and temper as well as of her personal appearance for except the miniature drawn four years ago (and she is now double that age nearly) I have no idea of even her aspect. When I am advised on these points, I can form some notion of her character and what way her dispositions or indispositions ought (to be) treated and though I will never interfere or thwart her mother yet I may perhaps be permitted to suggest as she (Lady B) is not obliged to follow my notions unless she likes which is not very likely. Is the Girl imaginative? At her present age I have an idea that I have many feelings and notions which people would not believe if I stated them now and therefore I may as well keep them to myself. Is she social or solitary, taciturn or talkative, fond

of reading or otherwise? And what is her tic? I mean her foible is she passionate? I hope that the Gods have made her anything save poetical. It is enough to have one such fool in a family.

Byron was forever searching for constant reassurances that Ada was well and the getting to know of her likes and dislikes helped him build up a picture in his head of what his little girl was growing up like, which helped him to form an attachment to her. Thinking about what kind of person his daughter was becoming may have helped Byron form a bond with Ada despite the many miles that parted them, but one thing he was certain of was that he did not want her to follow in his footsteps and be poetical; recognising what it had done to him, he had no desire for his daughter to suffer the same fate. That said, it is hard to imagine him being comfortable with the level of suppression she was enduring at home – he would have wanted her personality to flourish and for her to enjoy a series of happy friendships with other children. It is hard to imagine him condoning such strict restrictions on her thoughts, although he was pleased that her education was not being overlooked.

As well as gaining an understanding of Ada's personality and her likes and dislikes, it was important for him to know what she looked like, so Lady Byron provided him with a portrait of their daughter. She was a pretty girl with a pleasant smile and bright eyes. He treasured the picture and proudly put it on display, and when he heard the news that Ada had been taken ill, he was anxious to hear of her progress. In fact, his mind was so distracted with worry, he even stopped writing whilst Ada was ill and did not take up his pen again until he had received news of her full recovery. He waited impatiently for Augusta to write to him with updates; he wanted Lady Byron to know that he had suffered similar ailments when he was Ada's age and that she must keep an eye out for certain symptoms, lest it be an inherited condition. He was clearly worried and concerned enough with Ada's health to go to the trouble of expressing his concerns to Lady Byron. Byron had always had issues with his health in as much as he suffered headaches and became obsessed with his eating and appearance throughout his life, and any indication that his daughter could be the same must be highlighted and dealt with appropriately.

Lady Byron's mother, Lady Judith Noel, passed away in January 1822 (her father passed away in March 1825). In her will, she specifically stated that Ada was to have no dealings with her father, and that included looking upon the Albanian portrait, until she came of age, at which point she was free to make the decision herself as to whether she had any form of relationship with him. Although, in the unlikely event that Byron ever came knocking, there was little the family could have done to prevent any association he wished to have with his daughter. Lady Judith and Lord Byron had never got on; he fared much better with Sir Ralph, but his daughter's separation had cost him dear and the family suffered money problems as a result until Lady Noel inherited the Wentworth estate in 1815. She had been a devoted mother and grandmother and her death had a profound impact on Lady Byron and the young Ada. As Ada had a fractious relationship with her own mother and a non-existent relationship with her father, Judith had provided some form of family stability; she was an ever-present figure who could steady the ship. Now she was gone, Ada became even more isolated from the outside world. With no one now there to guide and advise Lady Byron on how to bring up a young girl, she started making more decisions that resulted in cutting Ada off even further. Any friends she did have were carefully vetted by Lady Byron before they were allowed to be established, and not many passed the strict list of requirements. Her friends usually came via friends of her mother's.

As it turned out, Ada never had to make the decision of whether she wanted a relationship with her estranged father, as he died two years after Judith, aged just 36 years old, in Missolonghi, Greece, whilst fighting for Greek independence from the Ottoman Empire.

He had volunteered to raise an army and they became known as the Byron Brigade. Ada was just 8 years old when her father passed away, and with him went the chance of her ever getting to know him.

When Byron died on 19 April 1824, he did not forget his daughter. On his death bed, he called out, 'Oh, my poor child. My dear Ada! My God! Could I but have seen her!'

It is easy for us to dismiss Byron as a terribly neglectful father but his anguish is plain to see. His behaviour during her birth was certainly questionable and he abandoned her at just four weeks old. But is it fair that we brand him a bad father when we consider the reasoning behind his decisions? For example, he never cut all lines of communication, even when his relationship with Lady Byron had completely broken down. He made sure he could get information regarding Ada either through friends or Augusta, which means that Lady Byron was happy to converse with them regarding her daughter. For all his faults, of which there were many, we cannot deny that he remained a concerned and devoted father and her wellbeing remained important to him up to his death.

It may seem strange to call a father who deserted his young child devoted, but it is clear from reading his letters that he had very good reasons for his actions. Byron knew he had to leave England following the break-up of his marriage; it had become too dangerous for him to remain and, whilst he was content to leave Lady Byron and cut ties with her, he was never willing to cut ties with Ada. He clearly never intended to turn his back on her completely but realised that he had to remove himself from her life for her own good. He recognised he had issues that caused concern, that he was susceptible to terrible mood swings and bouts of deep depression that sent him to some very dark places, and he had hoped to protect Ada from not just him as a person but also his reputation and everything that went with being the daughter of Lord Byron.

He understood the scrutiny that she would be under. If she was not in his care, then the hope was that she would be saved from any of the pitfalls and distresses that she would have to endure had she travelled with her father to Europe. He looked back at his own unhappy childhood and decided he wanted something better for his daughter and therefore made the decision to leave her in the care of her mother. Her health and wellbeing obviously meant a lot to him; she was always on his mind and he constantly looked for assurances that she was being well cared for. Her mental stability would have been of paramount concern for both parents and how her mind was developing was vital – could he spot any of the signs he had experienced? It was important for Lady Byron that he speak up if he did.

When he heard news of the suppression of his likeness at Kirkby Mallory, he sought legal advice to determine if this was allowed; it turned out it was, but knowing that she was not allowed to look at him, or even see his handwriting, must have hurt Byron deeply. After all, he had left Ada with Lady Byron and trusted she would bring her up in an acceptable manner – to find out he was being whitewashed from his daughter's life would have been alarming to him. Lady Byron was treading a fine line, for he could have made things much more difficult for her, but he chose to remove himself from their lives for the sake of their daughter.

When news of Lord Byron's death arrived in England three weeks later, it shocked many people. There were many questions to be answered such as how and why he had died. Many accusations were being thrown about amongst his friends and serious questions were being asked of his physicians, given the sudden nature of his passing. At the time, many suggested they should have bled Byron much earlier than they did. Although he refused, it is thought they should have insisted, as this was common practice at the time and a widely accepted form of treatment, but later medical experts have claimed it was the excessive bleeding that actually contributed to his death, along with an infection that he became too weak to fight, due to the lack of blood.

On his deathbed, Byron is claimed to have asked William Fletcher to bear a message to Ada. He lamented the fact that he never returned to England to see her before he headed to Greece but in reality, this could never had happened. The second he put a foot on English soil he would have been hounded, not to mention the resistance from Lady Byron and her mother. An autopsy followed the day after his death, at which time his heart was removed and placed in an urn. There was a legend that his heart had remained in Missolonghi, but this is in fact incorrect; it was reunited with his body prior to returning to England. Byron wanted to be buried in Greece, but the decision was made to return him home to England. On 25 May 1824, he was loaded onto the *Florida* and finally set sail for home, arriving on 29 June, after which he was taken up the Thames to London, where he lay in state for two days before he started his final journey on 12 July from Westminster to Hucknall Torkard in Nottinghamshire. Despite leaving the country under a cloud just a few years earlier, due to his hedonistic lifestyle, he was widely mourned amongst his peers and the public at large at home in England. He was a hero of the Greek people after fighting on their behalf in their war of independence and when Ada was told of her father's death, she is said to have wept.

Despite what had gone before, Lady Byron was devastated to learn of her husband's death, and she made the decision to keep her daughter away from the public outpouring of grief. Ada had no idea at the time how much her father was mourned. In true Lady Byron fashion, she was not as sympathetic as perhaps she should have been towards her daughter; she callously explained to Ada that she had no reason to be upset at the news and no right to grieve his loss, as she had no relationship with him, she did not know him, unlike her mother – her grief was more sincere.

As an 8-year-old child, Ada perhaps did not fully understand what her mother was saying to her. Of course, she understood that her father was dead, but she may have struggled with the idea that she would now never have an opportunity to meet him, never form her own opinions of him, and never truly know how much like him she was. All of a sudden, Byron became myth-like to Ada; she had no hard evidence to go on in terms of his character and now that he was dead, she was free to build up any picture she liked of him. To be fair, that can be said of his persona for everyone. At the point of his death, the Byron legend was created – people started to question whether all the rumours were true and without him alive to verify anything, the stories grew wilder and wilder.

All Ada had to go on was what other people had told her and, as a child, that was heavily filtered. It was only when she was older that she fully understood what and who her father was and by then it was too late. Her father was just a name, a shadow created by other people. She needed to see something tangible to place her father and his death in the context of her life, so Lady Byron allowed her to go and visit the ship that had transported her father's body back to England, but only after his remains had been removed and the vessel safely docked in London. After being refused burial at Westminster Abbey due to his questionable morality, Byron's cortege made its way from London to Nottinghamshire and Newstead Abbey. It would take until 1969 before he was recognised in Poet's Corner in the Abbey when, on 8 May, a white marble memorial plaque, inlaid with gold writing, was unveiled. It was given to the Abbey by the Poetry Society, and it reads:

Lord Byron, Died 19 April 1824 aged 36 at
Missolonghi, Greece.
But there is that within me which shall tire
Torture and Time, and breathe when I expire

The public outpouring of grief was palpable, as vast crowds lined the cortege's route with many openly grieving at the loss of the country's most successful poet. For all his past indiscretions, it would appear Byron had been truly loved by the English people. His body was treated with the greatest respect and as a peer of the realm, he was shown the reverence his status deserved and at each resting stage along the route people gathered to pay their final respects. When the funeral cortege arrived at its destination five days later, many more people queued up to file past the coffin as it lay in state, surrounded by the Byron coat of arms.

He was finally laid to rest next to his mother in the Byron family vault at the church of St Mary Magdalene in Hucknall Torkard, just a short distance from Newstead Abbey. The death of Lord Byron was shrouded in mystery and from his life sprang many myths and legends that have been talked about since. To the Greeks, he was a national hero; they even erected a statue in his honour and the King of Greece donated a marble plaque in recognition of his heroics during the Wars of Independence with Turkey, which stands near the Byron crypt in Hucknall. From the moment of his passing to the minute he was laid to rest, Ada was kept in complete ignorance. Her father's death may have had a huge impact on the public, but to her, it was a private matter that passed without any true understanding of what she had lost. Lady Byron had so far done her best to shield Ada from Byron's name and influence, but now he was dead, he became even more of a spectre, casting a shadow over their lives, as in death the Byron legend grew and the distinction between rumour and truth became more and more blurred.

With the death of her father came more freedom for Ada, and in 1826 she was finally able to join her mother on a visit to the continent. No doubt Lady Byron viewed this trip as an essential part of her daughter's education. Many young men of a similar rank undertook the Grand Tour of Europe and Ada was very fortunate that her mother was allowing her to do the same. She visited many of the places her father had done years earlier, including Lake Geneva and Italy, where she stayed in Genoa and Turin. It was an extensive trip that allowed the travelling party to fully immerse themselves in continental life, and they did not return to England until late 1827. Throughout her travels, Ada absorbed her surroundings; she took in everything she saw, heard, and smelt. A trip like this must have brought her closer to her father. Just as he had tried to get a sense of Ada's personality through objects and stories, she was doing the same by gazing upon the same beautiful Italian sunsets that he would have done. The places she visited, including the glacial summit of Mont Blanc, were a world away from her stifling life in England. The fresh open spaces must have brought her senses to life.

Upon her return home, Ada quickly settled back into the suffocating existence she had learned to endure, which must have been difficult now that she had had a taste of the wider world, experienced the wide-open spaces of Switzerland, and met new people with new attitudes. Her eyes and mind had been opened to new ideas and Ada wrote to her mother in February 1828 to declare she wanted to learn how to fly and that she was going to write a book called 'flyology', which would explain how she was going to achieve this. This was far from being a childish whim; she was deadly serious and was convinced she could achieve her goals as long as she applied herself properly. Despite Lady Byron's request that John Murray never publish anything her daughter had written, she was enthusiastic about Ada's latest venture. It was a fanciful idea but it was one that was rooted in scientific application. Ada was a methodical child and before she could even contemplate putting pen to paper, she needed to conduct a thorough set of precise experiments. She considered what materials she would need, what would work best in terms of durability, and what dimensions would be required in order to make sure everything was finely balanced. There was no margin for error. To help with this, she designed her very own flying room, in which she installed ropes, pulleys, and plenty of space to design her very own set of wings that would carry her up into the sky.

Ada was not the kind of child who would launch into a project like this with reckless abandon, and every aspect of the project was taken seriously and studied carefully. She devoted many hours to the study of the anatomy of birds, looking at how their wings worked and how she could apply what she learnt to her own ideas. Even at such a young age, we can see that Ada had the ability to think far beyond her capabilities and was light years ahead of her time. She had the intelligence to come up with ideas that were far beyond her young years and far beyond anything a girl should be thinking about. They would manifest themselves within her mindset and she took the time to think and consider each one individually, carefully deciding if an idea was worth pursuing.

All this work took place long before her mind turned to computers and her major scientific breakthrough. Ada was someone who was always looking for the next advancement; just when she had reached what others thought were the full competencies of a machine, she would then stop and think about how they could advance the technology even more to achieve bigger and better things, and she applied this logic to her flying aspirations. Not content with designing and using artificial wings, Ada wanted to go a step further, so she grappled with the possibility of applying steam power in an attempt to propel her skywards. Whilst her ideas stretched far beyond a girl of her age, the design of her flying machine had something of the childlike about it. She envisioned herself astride a large winged horse with the steam engines concealed within its belly. The steam generated would flap the wings, which would in turn lift the horse off the ground and into the sky. It is astonishing that a girl of 12 years old was able to set all this down on paper with diagrams as to how it would all work. She was quite clearly extremely gifted when it came to science and mathematics.

When Ada was working on a project, she totally immersed herself in her work, but all the talk of flying and building steam-powered flying horses, coupled with the continuing restrictions that were imposed upon her by Lady Byron, were beginning to take their toll on her, and soon her health became a major cause for concern. She had always been a sickly child – she suffered with headaches from an early age – but in 1829 she was going to suffer an illness that would prove debilitating and would bring to an end any ideas of flight and would halt her studies in their tracks. At first, it appeared that Ada was suffering with nothing more than a serious bout of measles, but her illness quickly manifested itself into something much more sinister, leaving her bedridden. The mystery illness quickly took hold and affected her sight and mobility, meaning she was quickly rendered blind and paralysed. It would take until mid-1830 before she showed any signs of recovery, and even then she was only able to walk on crutches.

As she grew older, the childlike ideas of steam-powered flying horses diminished and her true mathematical talents started to show themselves. When she was deemed strong enough to resume her studies, Lady Byron set about enrolling her on a new education path. Her first step was to enlist the help of men who were well-respected in their fields, so she engaged the services of the radical reformer and mathematician William Frend, and physician Dr William King. Both men were to instruct Ada further in maths and science. The emphasis on these subjects started now for Ada and she began to show a real interest and desire in learning more. It was also highly unlikely that either of these men would be dismissed for deviating from the syllabus. Ada's education stepped up a notch, and what she learned from these men gave her the foundation she needed to progress. Credit must be given to Lady Byron in that she encouraged her daughter to learn and that she gave her every opportunity to excel in her chosen fields, fields that she herself had shown a great interest in when she was younger. By giving Ada the best education, she would be in a position to show how sensible, logical, and intelligent she was. Lady Byron saw a talent in her daughter that needed to be nurtured correctly and it was her hope that these two esteemed men would help keep Ada on the straight and narrow, both morally and educationally.

But it was a frustrating time for Ada, as her health took a long time to fully return, which led to her spending many lonely weeks indoors by herself. She was unable to focus on her studies, so it was no surprise that her behaviour started to alter. She suddenly became a picky eater, confrontational and restless, rather like her father had done. She also started to rebel against her mother's treatment of her. Lady Byron's oppressive and overbearing nature had finally become too much for Ada to bear any longer. Her mother's need to control every aspect of her life became too much, but Ada had no outlet that she could offload her worries and frustrations on; her friends were of her mother's choosing and she had nowhere to turn. Lady Byron was adamant that Ada was to be brought up in the least Byronic way possible, but that was beginning to crush the spirit out of her daughter, to the point that she would have no personality at all. Ada was buckling under the weight of expectation, and she found trying to conform to her mother's idea of the model daughter unrealistic to maintain.

Lady Byron's obsession with proving she was nothing like her wayward husband and rooting out any potential insanity in Ada was just as bad at this point as it ever was. His death had not lessened that need in her and she remained desperate to distance herself from his behaviour. Byron's death had brought him back into the public's consciousness and to see him return home a hero must have upset Lady Byron, as the distress the marital break-up caused her was clearly still raw, so she tightened the reins on Ada even more. There was always a sense that Lady Byron had to constantly justify her reasons for leaving Byron; it was such a rare thing for a woman to do at that time that she had to go that extra mile to prove it was the right decision. Her reputation, and that of her daughter, had to be beyond reproach, so she threw weight and money behind lots of deserving causes, including setting up a school at Ealing Grove in 1833. But whilst Lady Byron was concerned with her reputation and good causes, she failed to see that her daughter was fast becoming a shadow of her former self. As well as battling her illness, she was tired of constantly being moved from one residence to another and of being spied upon by her tutors. All the people employed by her mother were expected to keep an eye on Ada and were required to report back anything that might cause alarm. Every slight move Ada made was to be noted, and some even invented stories to demonstrate they were being watchful of their charge. Ada dubbed these women 'The Furies' and she would come to hate them; they were figures of oppression and she would distrust them her whole life.

Ada and Lady Byron had never enjoyed a close mother/daughter relationship, and it was no wonder the relationship between the pair began to cool even further now that she was older – she was able to understand what damage her mother's behaviour was having on her. Ada's mood was low as she was not in a position to do anything to escape her mother, but things started to brighten up for her when a new tutor arrived to teach her shorthand. William Turner was about to awaken something in Ada and set her on a road to potential ruin and make Lady Byron's worst nightmare come true.

William and Ada made an instant connection; they were mutually attracted to each other and before long, their lessons were being replaced with secret meetings. They were always looking for ways in which they could be together and what they did in these private moments has been widely speculated on. Ada made the comment that they were as close as a man and woman could be without a full 'connexion'. Clearly there was a lot more than shorthand writing lessons going on, and how they managed to meet secretly without Lady Byron finding out is quite remarkable. 'The Furies' were not watching Ada as closely as they ought to have been, and that would soon come back to haunt them. Eventually, the young lovers were caught together, and the news soon made its way back to Lady Byron, but how long had this been going on and how serious was it? Was he in love with her, or was it her fortune and reputation he wanted? It was serious enough; Ada's morals had been compromised and unsurprisingly William was sacked on the spot and Ada put under even closer observation than she was before.

The relationship between tutor and pupil had awoken something deep within her; she had had a taste of freedom, passion, and love and now she had an idea of what life could be like if she could only escape her mother's beady eye. She decided enough was enough. She feared her mother no longer and so she made a dash from the house and headed straight to her lover's home, where they made plans to elope. Unfortunately for them, their plans were promptly discovered, and Ada was very quickly sent home to her extremely disappointed mother. We can only imagine the state Lady Byron was in when she discovered Ada's flight from home; she must have been livid. After all her hard work, Ada nearly undid it all with one foolish act.

Thankfully, disaster had been narrowly averted. Any act like this by any woman of Ada's social standing would have caused major ripples, but the fact that Lord Byron's daughter had behaved in such a manner would have set tongues wagging at a pace; this was by far the most Byronic thing Ada had ever done and proved that keeping her under restraint was not going to be as easy as Lady Byron had first thought. Every effort was made to cover this scandal up. Lady Byron was not going to allow Ada's virtue to be compromised in this manner, no matter how much distress it caused her to see her daughter lose all control of herself. Ada showed a desire for freedom and, even more worryingly, that she had a passionate nature. Lady Byron could not even contemplate these things and, despite her best efforts, Ada was proving to be her father's daughter. Perhaps if she hadn't had been so strict with Ada when she was younger, she would have had no need or desire to rebel.

In May 1833, at the age of 17, Ada was presented to King William V and Queen Adelaide. Also in attendance were the Duke of Wellington and Lord Melbourne. Both had had a dislike of Byron but were keen to know his daughter and see how she had turned out. Ada did not like being the object of curiosity; she spent her home life under scrutiny she did not wish to suffer that treatment in society too – the idea of being looked and talked about filled her with horror.

Ada had had a near miss with her tutor and was lucky Lady Byron had decided to forgive her and move on from this show of indiscretion. What Ada needed now was to return to her studies. Lady Byron agreed that her daughter had to get back on track in terms of her educational development; it would do Ada good to have her logical brain rebalanced, she had experienced more than enough excitement for the time being. It was important now more than ever that Lady Byron steered her daughter in the right direction. That direction was Marylebone and the home of eminent scientist Charles Babbage, and it would be through him that Ada's life would change forever.

Chapter Three

Ada, the Mathematical Genius

Born on 26 December 1791 in London, Charles Babbage, who is known as 'the father of computers', was the son of a wealthy banker. He married Georgiana Whitmore in 1814 and the marriage was very happy, despite his father having serious concerns about the union. From 1810, Babbage attended Trinity College, Cambridge, and it was here that he formed the Analytical Society with fellow scientists John Herschel and George Peacock. By 1816, he had been elected as fellow of the Royal Society in London. He was later appointed Lucasian Professor of Mathematics at Cambridge. He commented that achieving this role was the only true moment of recognition he received throughout his career, despite all the ground-breaking scientific work he did; he craved recognition and, in his opinion, received very little.

Babbage was the most eminent mathematician and inventor of his age, and was known as a 'gentleman of science' – in other words, he was a man of means who was able to support himself and his family whilst working in the field of science. The occupation of scientist as we understand it today was not established or recognised in the Victorian era, but Babbage was rich enough to pursue his interests without the worry of needing to earn a living. He was a very innovative man, and his full list of inventions is extensive and covers a multitude of disciplines; amongst other ideas, he came up with a black box recorder that could be installed on trains, which had the ability to monitor certain conditions prior to railway disasters, very much like the instruments used in aeroplanes today that can provide vital information during the investigation of an accident. Sticking with trains, he also invented failsafe quick-release couplings for railway carriages and a speedometer to name just a few.

He was a proud and principled man and was often outspoken. He was considered by many to be an eccentric who longed for reward and validation for his work; sadly, he felt that, he received very little of either, although he did decline a knighthood and baronetcy, which, it could be argued, is the highest level of recognition someone could achieve. His reputation following his death is still as strong now as it was when he was alive. When he died in October 1871 at the age of 79, it was reported that his brain was split in two; one half was sent to the Hunterian Museum of the Royal College of Surgeons in London and the other half was sent to the Science Museum, where it can be viewed.

Following his death, it was his son Henry who donated the brain, in the hope that would help with 'the advancement of human knowledge and the good of the human race'. Babbage was often critical of the British scientific establishment and frequently fell out with and offended those who he relied on for support. But he was considered a genius, albeit a rude one, and people were often reluctant to work with him. Sadly, in 1827, Babbage suffered the devastating loss of his beloved wife, two of his children, and his father, and so in 1828, he decided to relocate to 1 Dorset Street, Marylebone. This would become the new family home and also the venue for his legendary Saturday soirees. He would invite the great and the good of London's society to converse on the latest scientific discoveries that were being developed across the continent. For him, it was an opportunity to showcase his own inventions, and the one that his name would become famous for was showcased here in 1833.

The Victorian age is renowned as being one of innovation and progression. It was a time that saw massive advancements in science and technology, which would revolutionise the world. Industry in Britain was developing at a fast pace and these changes would go on to alter the lives of many, both rich and poor, and whilst the majority of people embraced the changes and could appreciate the benefits new technology could bring, there were others who felt intimidated and scared of what these new ideas could mean. On 15 June 1833, Babbage held one of his renowned evening soirees. He invited his guests to witness his latest invention, which he had called the Difference Engine. The Difference Engine that was on show that night at Babbage's home was only a fraction of what the completed engine would look like, a prototype, if you will, but it gave those in attendance a glimpse of what a contraption like his could potentially achieve once it was fully built. Fully completed, it would be the most advanced technological machine that the Victorian world had ever seen, and in attendance that night to witness the Difference Engine's debut were Ada and her mother.

As she stood amongst the throng of people, Ada took in the Difference Engine in all its glory; however, the difference between her and her fellow guests was that she was able to see and appreciate what the engine could potentially be capable of doing – if Babbage could get it built to its full capacity, it could change the world. It captivated Ada. Even at such a young age, she was showing signs of her future potential; thanks to her tutors, she already had the foresight to understand complex and intricate scientific designs and process what she was witnessing and apply it to daily life. The ideas that Babbage was coming up with were feasible to Ada, they were tangible inventions that had the ability to revolutionise thought and life, just like her steam-powered flying horse. She could appreciate the usefulness and usability of the Difference Engine and that appealed to her. Ada was unique in this respect – not only was she young to have this level of understanding, she was also a woman, to whom the scientific arena was not always so welcoming, but Babbage saw beyond her gender and tender years and could fully appreciate her talents. That evening marked the start of a remarkable lifelong friendship between the two of them. Babbage was a tricky person to get on with and Ada could be stubborn, so it would not always be plain sailing, but they would work closely together on this and future projects; she would turn to him for guidance and advice when it came to her work. Clearly Babbage saw the potential in Ada and appreciated that her mind was something unique. He was happy to share his plans and ideas for the Difference Engine with her and she in turn would study them in minute detail to fully understand its workings and its potential to change the world.

Babbage had many interests, including a fascination for data tables, and he would spend many an hour looking over them to find errors. At this time, these tables were produced manually and often contained human errors, which is natural, but these tables were highly important in navigation, particularly at sea, and so any error could cause serious miscalculations, which in turn could have catastrophic consequences. In order to eradicate these errors, Babbage decided to create a machine that would eliminate the need for human intervention and thus limit the number of errors that would occur. This would be achieved by using the mathematical method of finite differences and it was from these ideas that the Difference Engine was born.

His designs were impressive and people were so fascinated and excited at what Babbage was proposing that in 1822, he was awarded £1,000 by the British government to build his machine. He immediately set to work on a prototype and, in 1823, employed the services of Joseph Clement, a master tool maker and draftsman who was well-respected for his skills in precision engineering, to build the engine. Sadly, the pair fell out, but knowing what we do of Babbage's character, it is no wonder. Naturally, Clement required certain tools to undertake a job of this size, but these cost a lot of money and, back then, the workman would own the tools at the end of the job, rather than the master who paid for them. This angered Babbage and, coupled with his request for the construction to be relocated from Clement's workshops to premises nearer to his own home being refused, they fell out.

Babbage refused to pay any compensation to Clement for the move, so it is little wonder Clement was so angered; he decided enough was enough and he could no longer work with Babbage, so he downed his tools, sacked his workforce, and a full-size version of the machine was never completed. However, a demonstration model was built in 1832, and it was this engine that Ada saw that evening in 1833. She became obsessed with what she had witnessed that night and often persuaded scientist and friend Mary Somerville to accompany her to Babbage's home so she could see and watch the machine in action. The meetings with Babbage and his engine sparked something within Ada and she decided she wanted to expand her mathematical knowledge even further, so in 1834, she started taking lessons with Mary Somerville. Mary Somerville was a renowned Scottish scientist and mathematician who became one of the first female Honorary Members of the Royal Astronomical Society. She was very well-respected within the scientific world and even held rank with men. She was considered to be one of the age's most prominent scientists; in 1834, she became the first person in history to be mentioned as a scientist in print. Luckily for Ada, she was also a very good friend of Lady Byron's and so the role of maths teacher seemed a natural one. Mary and Ada formed a friendship that would prove to be long lasting. Mathematics became a subject that Ada was happy to fully immerse herself in – she was a dedicated pupil and was always happy to engage in her studies, finally, much to Lady Byron's relief. Her daughter seemed settled in a subject that would nourish her mind and keep her thoughts away from young men and other exciting things. It looked like she had beaten the Byron curse.

If it had been built to its full size, the Difference Engine would have been a hand-cranked mechanical calculator that would have been able to calculate polynomial functions, which would then have eliminated the need for multiplication and division to produce numerical tables. Instead, it would be able to use simple arithmetic of addition and subtraction that could run indefinitely without any errors occurring. A proud Babbage announced to Humphrey Davy, the President of the Royal Society, that he had invented and partly built a mathematical machine that had the ability to produce a table of all the prime numbers between 0 and 10,000,000. Fully built, it would have contained over 25,000 parts and weighed a staggering four tonnes. It is possible to see a portion of the Difference Engine as per Babbage's original designs in the Science Museum in London today. Following a project in 1991 to build the machine, in 2000, they added the printer function that Babbage's original drawings indicated.

With the working relationship between Babbage and Clement over, the project to build the Difference Engine was a non-starter, but Babbage was not to be put off and soon turned his attention to a much grander engine. It would be this engine that Ada's name would later become synonymous with.

The Analytical Engine is described by Britannica's encyclopedia as a general-purpose, fully program-controlled, automatic mechanical digital computer. It was a steam-powered general-purpose programmable digital computer and work on it started in mid-1839. It was a far more complex engine than the earlier Difference Engine. It would be bigger and more powerful, it was designed to work out any calculation that was set and then to deliver instructions, as well as having a memory unit to store the numbers. All this functionality and the capability to remember and predict results meant that it became the precursor to the modern-day computer, although at the time, it was unclear just how important a machine it would turn out to be. It had the ability to modify its own calculation whilst running and was able to pause mid-process and consider the values it had already calculated to choose between two possible next steps. By being able to do this, it had the ability to work the calculations out as it went along.

The machine was programmed using punched cards, like the Jacquard Loom, which used a similar method in its production of patterned material; the numbers were entered onto each card, which were then placed into separate decks – this would be the program and gave starting values for the computations. A complex mechanism allowed the machine to repeat a deck of cards to execute a loop. The hardware was known as the 'mill', that is to say, the actual physical machine and its components, and once built, the central processing unit would reach as tall as 15ft, and the memory, which was known as the store, would be able to hold fifty-digit numbers and would be as long as 20ft. Other components included a printer, card punch, and a graph plotter. Babbage estimated it would take three minutes to multiply two twenty-digit numbers. We recognise these components, as they are all present in the modern-day computer.

Unsurprisingly, the failure to build the promising Difference Engine, despite having the funding to do so, meant there was a lack of enthusiasm for the Analytical Engine from the British scientific establishment. In his frustration at this lack of ambition, Babbage turned to the continent for help in the hope he would secure the necessary funds. He finally had a breakthrough in 1840, when he was invited to Turin, Italy, where he was asked to give a lecture on the principles of the machine. He also went on to discuss the progress Italy was making in terms of its scientific achievements, as they felt they were lagging behind the French and saw the workings of the Analytical Engine as an opportunity to help advance them. In the audience was Captain Luigi Federico Menabrea, an Italian mathematician who, in October 1842, published his first-hand account of the engine in French, based on what he had noted at Babbage's lecture. His paper first appeared in an edition of *Bibliotheque Universalle de Geneve*. Babbage discussed the Analytical Engine with the Italians, but they failed to fully comprehend the significance of it and no funding was forthcoming.

Menabrea's report failed to ignite much interest either at home or abroad, so scientist and inventor Charles Wheatstone turned to Ada to see if she would be willing to translate Menabrea's article into English. She agreed. The request came at the perfect time for Ada, as she was struggling to settle her mind to one specific task; she was trying to concentrate on too many different projects at once, which left her feeling unsettled. Her friends urged her to concentrate on one thing at a time and it was at this point she decided to devote her time to the Analytical Engine and the translation of Menabrea's notes. With this new focus, Ada came alive with the challenge and threw herself into her work. It did not take Ada long to complete the translation and, after only a matter of months, she referred her work back to Wheatstone.

Many questioned if a woman, not to mention a countess, could be deemed capable of writing such a paper that was to be read predominantly by men. Clearly Wheatstone had no qualms in asking her to do the translation and Babbage went further and invited Ada to write a series of detailed notes on the Analytical Engine. Both men had faith in her abilities to understand what she was working on, which must have boosted her confidence. She took time to consider Babbage's offer. Ada, who was married by this time, would have likely talked it over with her husband William, and maybe even Lady Byron. There was much to think about because the Analytical Engine was such complex machine. Ada was a conscientious person so she had to truly believe it would work and not turn out to be some fantasy machine that Babbage had dreamed up, which, when it came to it, was too far-fetched to work in any coherent way. After all, there was a distinct lack of interest for the Analytical Engine in England, with the government thinking it of little or no scientific interest at all; could this have been because they did not think it viable, or had they simply refused to fund it because of the lack of end product with the Difference Engine? More than likely, it was the latter, for there was no questioning Babbage's ability to invent useful, worthwhile machines.

The other aspect Ada had to consider was the added pressure that if she was unsuccessful and showed she had inherited neither of her parents' genius, what would that mean for her in terms of her role in society, would she just become another wife and mother? That does not seem fitting for Lord Byron's daughter, surely she was destined for greatness. She risked the possibility of ridicule – people had been waiting for a moment to compare her to her father and this was it. She had to weigh up if she was brave enough to put herself out there and risk failure. All of these reasons had to be considered and, despite any reservations she had, and probably with a gentle nudge from her husband, she decided to accept the commission and began work on it in spring 1843.

Ada did not come up with a plan of action; there was no methodical way of working. Instead, she dived right in and very quickly realised her notes were a lot longer than the original paper. Ada had clearly grasped the workings of the Analytical Engine a lot better than the Italians had, and she raced through the paper, adding notes upon notes, her mind going into overdrive with all the ideas that were fighting for her attention. Babbage encouraged Ada and was getting very excited with her work; he even suggested sending them to Prince Albert to read them over before they were published. Albert had previously shown a keen interest in Ada and her work but thankfully she managed to talk Babbage out of this and instead turned her concentration back to the machine and what it could potentially do.

Despite Ada's pleas not to share her notes, Prince Albert did visit Babbage at his home in Dover Street to witness the Analytical Engine, but in the end, he decided against offering his support for the project. Babbage was not asked to participate in the Great Exhibition of 1851, and it is said that Queen Victoria was not keen on Ada, given that Prince Albert had shown such a keen interest in her. It is well-known that the Queen was jealous when it came to her husband showing interest in other women; whether it was jealousy or the fact that Ada was a woman working in a man's domain that offended her, we do not know. Ada and her mother are mentioned in a diary entry of the Queen's in 1839 when she notes she held a discussion about the two women with Lord Melbourne, but that was probably because he was their kinsman rather than for any other reason. Ada and the Queen did meet in 1838 when William was granted the Earldom of Lovelace, but other than that, it would appear Ada never crossed paths with the monarch.

The first aspect Ada looked at were the notable differences between the earlier Difference Engine and the Analytical Engine. This is noted as *Note A* in the paper and was aimed at explaining the significance of the Analytical Engine, although this proved difficult as there was no real comparative machine – she could not even draw on the Difference Engine as a reference point as that had never been built. All she had to refer back to were the original drawings and the prototype. Moving on, Ada then proceeded to explain what the actual build of the Analytical Engine would be; again, she was armed with Babbage's drawings, and she started by describing the different parts of the engine, the store, the mill, and the use of the punch cards. It was whilst she was working on the use of punch cards that she had her lightbulb moment and realised that the capability of the Analytical Engine could be more far-reaching than either she or Babbage ever realised. It was more than a mere calculator and you could use more than just numbers to calculate a result – it might even be possible to use it to play music, she claimed in her extensive notes:

> Supposing, for instance, that the fundamental relations of pitched sounds in the science of harmony and of musical composition were susceptible of such expression and adaptations, the engine might compose elaborate and scientific pieces of music of any degree of complexity or extent.

This is an amazing leap by Ada to envisage that the engine could be capable of such things. Babbage himself had never come to this conclusion, which shows Ada's understanding of the Analytical Engine was so in-depth she could imagine much greater things.

The most famous of Ada's contributions is *Note G*. She included a way in which the machine could be used to calculate the Bernoulli numbers, in which you may use the first number to calculate the second, the second the third, and so on. There are lots of ways to calculate these numbers and Ada did not choose the easiest method, but she saw that the Analytical Engine was capable of doing so. She set down how the computation of the Bernoulli numbers could be fetched from 'the store' used in the calculation 'mill' and moved back again, according to the instructions on the cards.

The particular program would have been a deck of punched cards that caused the machine to make successive changes; the moving on of the numbers is indicative of the Bernoulli method. *Note G* is the cumulation of Ada's paper and pages of detailed explanations on how the engine worked show her obsessive attention to detail and her ability to see the bigger picture of what the engine could achieve. Ada was a perfectionist and would go over and over certain aspects of its mechanisms to ensure she fully understood what it was capable of. But she went one step further and, rather than limiting the engine to just mathematical calculations, she observed that it could act on things other than numbers if those things satisfied certain mathematical rules, for example, musical notes and algebra.

The table used to show the calculation at each stage is now considered to be the first computer program and earns Ada Lovelace the accolade of being the world's first computer programmer. Within these notes, she had created the first computer algorithm. She had faith in what she was writing about, and her reasons were to be justified years after her death when they were used in a matter of life and death for her country.

Ada stated that 'the Analytical Engine has no pretentions whatever to originate anything. It can do whatever we know how to order it to perform.' It was this statement that Alan Turing later argued against in his paper, calling it *Lady Lovelace's Objection*. Ada's work on the Analytical Engine was an extraordinary achievement that was probably understood and recognised by very few people at the time. To this day, algebra, mathematics, logic, and a little philosophy are the unchanging principles of the general use computer; the fact that Ada was using these principles so many years before the first computer was built is staggering.

Many questioned Ada's mathematical abilities, but she did not just simply stumble across these mathematical quandaries, she applied her knowledge and worked hard to fully understand what her findings meant. She wrote frequently to Babbage to update him on her progress and they conversed regularly about her findings, but it must be understood that this was not a case of Ada being the pupil, applying other people's ideas to her own work, and Babbage being the teacher. Granted, she may have asked for reassurance that what she was doing was viable, but ultimately it was Ada who was leading the way in setting down on paper these calculations.

After several months of hard work, the final paper was ready to be published in *Taylor's Scientific Memoirs* in August 1843. It was signed AAL (Augusta Ada Lovelace) and of its sixty-six pages, forty-one were Ada's additional notes. She added so much extra material in her annotations that it more than doubled the original piece. Despite the remarkable work by Ada, there was some bad feeling surrounding the publication. Still disgruntled about the lack of home support, Babbage wanted to add a note to the paper about the non-existent support from the British government, and whilst Ada did not object to this being included, she did not want it to be attached to her name or her notes. Wheatstone was of the same mind and did not want the statement attached to Ada either, and he offered to sign the document instead. Babbage wanted the statement to be published unsigned, which would then have made it look like they were the thoughts of Ada, so naturally she refused, but Babbage was still adamant he would not back down. He even went as far as writing to Ada requesting that she remove her notes altogether from the publication.

A request like this must have shattered Ada; she had spent so much time and devoted so much of herself to this work that this felt like betrayal, so she refused Babbage's request. He, on the other hand, could not understand her grievance. Surely Babbage had not used Ada. Did her name mean more to him than her actual talent, and was she just a platform for him to dole out his poisonous words? It is hard to imagine this, as there was such a warm friendship between them, but whatever the reasons were, she refused to let it derail her plans. Instead, she came up with a list of demands that Babbage had to agree to. Her main point was that she was to handle all the discussion when it came to the Analytical Engine and its funding.

The notes were finally published in *Taylor's Scientific Memoirs* and were well received, but for all of Ada's efforts, it did not raise enough interest and no offers of funding were received. Babbage's tirade was published in the sister publication *Philosophical Magazine*; it went unsigned. Babbage was clearly pleased with Ada's work and described her as an 'Enchantress of Numbers' but he turned down her offer to get involved in the funding and construction of the engine. Regardless of this professional disagreement, the two remained friends but did not work together again. The publication of the notes had given Ada her own independent identity. She had finally broken the Byron chains that had bound her all her life, she had achieved something in her own right. By this time, she was married and known as Ada, Countess of Lovelace, and it would be that name that she would become famous under, the Byron ghost finally laid to rest.

Lady Byron must have been relieved to see her daughter applying her knowledge to such a logical task, but you could not keep the poetic side of Ada's nature down for long, and she did claim the 'Analytical Engine weaves algebraic patterns just as the Jacquard Loom weaves flowers and leaves', a poetic statement her father would have been proud of and one her mother would have worried over!

Ada was married a few years after the first meeting with Babbage. Her mother felt she needed to settle down in a bid to curb any exciting thoughts she may have been harbouring; whilst her interest in the Difference Engine was encouraging and mentally stimulating, it was felt that Ada's personal life needed more stability, and the best way to achieve this was to settle into marriage and have children. Given the disastrous nature of her own marriage, Lady Byron must have been apprehensive when it came to her daughter marrying. It would take a kind and considerate man to marry Ada; he would need to be patient and understanding of her health and someone who would share her passion for science. As it turned out, there was just the man for Ada.

Chapter Four

Marriage to William and Motherhood

In early 1835, Ada suffered a complete mental and nervous breakdown at the family home of Mary Somerville. It was suggested the cause of the illness was down to the excitement of the past year, which had proved to have been too much for her. Despite her protests that she wanted to remain in London, she was sent to Brighton to recover, and whilst she was convalescing there, the decision was made that it was time Ada took a husband.

The topic of marriage was a tricky one. Lady Byron would have been desperate for Ada to choose the right kind of man to be her husband, considering the torment she had suffered during her marriage and subsequent split. The last thing Lady Byron would have wanted was for Ada to experience an unhappy marriage like she had. She would have been anxious that Ada did not go through the same experience, for if she did, the effect on her mental stability could have been catastrophic. It was of paramount importance that the right man was chosen, and the more unlike Lord Byron he was, the better. What Ada needed was a sensible older man of good birth with similar interests to her own, someone who could keep her calm and steady should the need arise.

It would take a special man to agree to marry Ada Byron; after all, she had a certain kind of reputation, not just through her name but through her own behaviour. She had health issues and an earlier indiscretion to explain away, and she was still a figure of interest – even years after her father's death, she still demanded a certain level of scrutiny. All of these factors would have to be considered by any perspective suitor before an offer could be made. Her future groom would have to be of an understanding nature, with a capacity for forgiveness, and who was willing to overlook her past indiscretions. He would also have to be a sensitive man and accept that her health was a constant battle, as she was vulnerable physically as well as mentally. He would have to be willing to nurse her through any bout of illness and be patient whilst he did. All of these issues could be readily accepted if he truly loved Ada; however, one aspect of his married life that he would have little control over was the realisation there would be a third person in the marriage, Lady Byron. This would have been non-negotiable and he would have to understand and take into consideration her feelings when decisions needed to be made regarding Ada. Luckily for Lady Byron, there was such a man who was willing to take on her daughter and all the baggage she came with, and that man was William King.

William King was born on 21 February 1805, which made him ten years older than Ada. He was the eldest son and heir of Peter King, 7th Baron King, and Lady Hester Fortescue. He was Eton- and Cambridge-educated and was destined for a career in politics. Sadly, he was treated terribly by his mother following the early death of his father; she gave away vast parts of the estate to her younger and preferred son, Peter John Locke King, who later became a well-known politician. She isolated William from his younger siblings and cruelly cut him off from his family. There is no clear evidence as to why she chose to behave in this manner towards her eldest son and there is nothing in William's character to suggest he would have been deserving of this treatment. We can only assume that she was jealous of William and the trappings he enjoyed as the eldest son, which she would have much preferred to be passed on to the younger son, although there never seemed to be any ill feeling between the brothers over their mother's behaviour.

William held many titles in his life. At birth, he was known as the Honourable William King and when he succeeded to the barony in 1833, following the death of his father, he was created Lord King. The titles of Viscount Ockham and Earl of Lovelace were bestowed on him in 1838, and he became Lord-Lieutenant of Surrey in 1840, a post which he held until his death in 1893. He was admitted as a Fellow of the Royal Society on 25th November 1841 and also held the post of secretary to the governor of the Ionian isles.

Ada and William met at a ball that was being held at Weston House, the Warwickshire home of the textile industrialist Sir George Philips and his wife, Lady Sarah-Ann. It was Lady Phillips who first introduced them that evening; they danced together and, by all accounts, there was an instant connection. Despite there being a significant age gap, this potential love match was encouraged on all sides, and he proposed just one week after their initial meeting. Ada did not hesitate in accepting his offer, realising that he was a respectable man of means. William was also a friend of Woronzow Grieg, the son of Mary Somerville, which meant they shared some acquaintances. This would have given Ada a sense of reassurance, given her close friendship with Mary, and trust would have been a major factor for Ada when considering her future husband.

Grieg was keen to encourage William to ask for Ada's hand in marriage, and they must have been considered a good match by those around them. William would have known who Ada was before he met her, he would have been aware of her family history and was prepared to accept the tribulations that went with that. He appears to have been keen to marry Ada. Lady Byron had already made him aware of her daughter's past indiscretions with her tutor and thankfully he was willing to overlook that, based on a promise from Lady Byron that Ada would be on her best behaviour after she was married and would settle down and became a model wife. William was pleased to learn that Lady Byron held sway over her daughter; he must have felt he needed that extra support in managing Ada and ensuring the first few years of married life were happy – all of a sudden, that third person in the marriage seemed like a good idea. William was a keen admirer of Lord Byron; we can only assume that Lady Byron was happy with this, as she thought William a good choice as a husband for Ada.

Presumably, she saw this as a positive thing, and she may even have encouraged this admiration to come to the fore in an attempt to teach Ada about her father.

It was considered the right time to approach the subject of Lord Byron with Ada. She was now a married woman and deemed beyond the reaches of immorality. Byron, it would appear, could no longer impact his daughter's conscience. William was probably considered by Lady Byron as a man who would be sympathetic when it came to talking to Ada about her father. She would certainly not have sanctioned the marriage if she had any doubts that he was going to support him when it came to the subject of the Byrons' failed marriage. William had attended Trinity College Cambridge like Byron, enjoyed his poetry, and relished the chance to marry his daughter. Marriage was a big step to take but, from Ada's perspective, she saw it as an opportunity to escape her mother's constant gaze and controlling behaviour. She thought William was a nice and pleasant man, he didn't bowl her over or sweep her off her feet, but she accepted that a love match for a woman of her station was a rare thing, and she should be grateful he was well-respected and would be kind to her.

The couple were married at the home of Lady Byron at Fordhook in Ealing, on 8 July 1835. Their first week as a married couple was spent at William's seat at Ockham Park before heading to Ashley Coombe in Somerset. William had spent time and money ensuring Ashley Coombe was restored and enlarged in time for their honeymoon – he wanted to create a romantic country home for them both to enjoy. The estate sat nestled in amongst a wood that overlooked the Bristol Channel. It had Italianate terraced gardens and a network of tunnels that were used by tradesmen so that they could not be seen arriving by the house guests. It would seem William took great care in creating a private home that Ada could retreat to; he even had a bath house built into the cliff so that she could bathe privately and escape the outside world. He was sensitive to the fact that his wife had a need for seclusion, for there were times when she needed to retreat to the privacy of her home to deal with illness.

If Ada had hoped married life would finally be her chance for freedom, she was sadly mistaken. The marriage settlement was rather attractive for William and was made up of £16,000 from Lady Byron's own dowry of £20,000, £14,000 added by Lady Byron herself, and £30,000 would be raised in rent from the Wentworth estates in the future. From this vast amount, Ada was given just £300 as a yearly allowance and from this this she had to pay for her maids, her clothes, and other expenses. It would appear that William was keeping his wife on a tight rein in terms of money; whether this was at her mother's suggestion or not, we can't be certain, but yet again we see the control and suppression of Ada. She was quite clearly not to be trusted with much more – was the fear she would gamble it away or spend it on unnecessary frivolities? Was she ever going to be allowed to enjoy the nice things in life without any restraint? We must question why she was treated this way. Maybe William was following orders from Lady Byron – had she filled his head with stories from her own marriage as a warning that if he granted Ada too much liberty, she would bring ruin upon them? She was definitely being punished for the sins of her father, as she had very rarely given any indication that she would descend into madness if she was given something fun to enjoy. She must have felt a certain level of frustration to find she had just swapped one eagle-eyed observer for another; it must have seemed she was never going to have the freedom to live the life she wanted.

At the time of her daughter's marriage, Lady Byron commissioned a portrait of Ada by Mrs Margaret Carpenter. The artist decided to dress her subject in an off-white gown and pull her hair away from her face, revealing the broad jawline that she shared with her father. Ada's stance mimicked that of her father's in his famous Albanian portrait. Ada hated her portrait with a passion, but Lady Byron loved it. Despite spending all of her upbringing trying to distance Ada from her father, Lady Byron now seemed to be drawing attention to the fact that Ada was Byron's daughter. She had chosen to draw people's attention to this fact in a very visual way; there was no escaping the likeness between father and daughter, and it was there for everyone to see. The only reason Lady Byron could now be drawing upon the similarities was that she must now have felt safe enough to draw that comparison, but what she hoped to gain from this behaviour we do not know. Why now would the comparison be a favourable one? Was she showing the world what a wonderful mother she had been, that despite all the troubles of her marriage to the most hedonistic of men, she had managed to raise Ada into a fine young woman who had married well? This portrait appears to be a large pat on the back for Lady Byron's parenting skills. She may have been proud of the woman Ada had turned into but she was going to take all the plaudits for achieving that.

Throughout their relationship, it feels as though there is an underlying unease that Lady Byron had an ulterior motive when it came to making important decisions for her daughter. It is almost contrived and never feels like any decision was made without her fully assessing the impact it would have on her and her reputation. This may be a harsh assessment of Lady Byron, and it is understandable that she needed to protect herself against the gossips, but as Ada got older, surely the need to justify her decisions diminished. There is no denying the fact it cannot have been an easy task bringing up a child in such circumstances, but you do get a sense that Ada was never allowed to forget how much her mother had sacrificed for her. Of course, Ada had never asked her to – she never asked to be born the daughter of Lord Byron – but it feels like she spent most of her life apologising for it.

That said, Lady Byron did honour the wishes of her mother of waiting until Ada was married before she should be allowed to receive some of her father's belongings. The main item that was eventually handed over was the Albanian portrait; finally free from its green

Right: Ada aged seventeen.

Below: Ada aged four.

Ada aged seven, by Alfred D'Orsay.

Ada by Alfred Edward Chalon, 1840.

Ada by Margaret Carpenter, 1836.

Ada daguerreotype by Antoine Claudet, 1850.

Left: Ada sitting at the piano by Henry Phillips, 1852.

Below: Annabella Milbanke.

Charles Babbage.

Augusta Leigh.

Lady Anne Blunt, Ada's daughter.

Above left: Lady Caroline Lamb by Thomas Lawrence.

Above right: Lord Byron in Albanian costume.

Diagram for the computation by the Engine of the Numbers of Bernoulli. See Note G. (page 722 *et seq.*)

Number of Operation.	Nature of Operation.	Variables acted upon.	Variables receiving results.	Indication of change in the value on any Variable.	Statement of Results.	Data						Working Variables.							Result Variables.			
						$^1V_1$	$^1V_2$	$^1V_3$	$^0V_4$	$^0V_5$	$^0V_6$	$^0V_7$	$^0V_8$	$^0V_9$	$^0V_{10}$	$^0V_{11}$	$^0V_{12}$	$^0V_{13}$	B_1 $^0V_{21}$	B_3 $^0V_{22}$	B_5 $^0V_{23}$	B_7 $^0V_{24}$
						1	2	n														
1	×	$^1V_2 \times ^1V_3$	$^1V_4, ^1V_5, ^1V_6$		$= 2n$				$2n$	$2n$	$2n$											
2	−	$^1V_4 - ^1V_1$	$^2V_4$		$= 2n - 1$				$2n-1$													
3	+	$^1V_5 + ^1V_1$	$^2V_5$		$= 2n + 1$					$2n+1$												
4	÷	$^2V_5 \div ^2V_4$	$^1V_{11}$		$= \dfrac{2n-1}{2n+1}$											$\dfrac{2n-1}{2n+1}$						
5	÷	$^1V_{11} \div ^1V_2$	$^2V_{11}$		$= \dfrac{1}{2}\cdot\dfrac{2n-1}{2n+1}$											$\dfrac{1}{2}\cdot\dfrac{2n-1}{2n+1}$						
6	−	$^1V_{13} - ^2V_{11}$	$^1V_{13}$		$= -\dfrac{1}{2}\cdot\dfrac{2n-1}{2n+1} = A_0$											0		$-\dfrac{1}{2}\cdot\dfrac{2n-1}{2n+1}$				
7	−	$^1V_3 - ^1V_1$	$^1V_{10}$		$= n - 1 (= 3)$										$n-1$							
8	+	$^1V_2 + ^0V_7$	$^1V_7$		$= 2 + 0 = 2$							2										
9	+	$^1V_6 + ^1V_7$	$^1V_{11}$		$= \dfrac{2n}{2} = A_1$						$2n$					$\dfrac{2n}{2} = A_1$						
10	×	$^1V_{21} \times ^1V_{11}$	$^1V_{12}$		$B_1 \cdot \dfrac{2n}{2} = B_1 A_1$											0	$B_1 \dfrac{2n}{2} = B_1 A_1$					
11	+	$^1V_{12} + ^1V_{13}$	$^1V_{13}$		$-\dfrac{1}{2}\cdot\dfrac{2n-1}{2n+1} + B_1 \cdot \dfrac{2n}{2}$												0	$\left\{-\dfrac{1}{2}\cdot\dfrac{2n-1}{2n+1} + B_1\dfrac{2n}{2}\right\}$	B_1			
12	−	$^1V_{10} - ^1V_1$	$^2V_{10}$		$= n - 2 (= 2)$										$n-2$							
13	−	$^2V_6 - ^1V_1$	$^3V_6$		$= 2n - 1$						$2n-1$											
14	+	$^1V_1 + ^1V_7$	$^2V_7$		$= 2 + 1 = 3$							3										
15	÷	$^3V_6 \div ^2V_7$	$^1V_8$		$= \dfrac{2n-1}{3}$								$\dfrac{2n-1}{3}$									
16	×	$^1V_8 \times ^2V_{11}$	$^3V_{11}$		$= \dfrac{2n}{2}\cdot\dfrac{2n-1}{3}$								0			$\dfrac{2n}{2}\cdot\dfrac{2n-1}{3}$						
17	−	$^3V_6 - ^1V_1$	$^4V_6$		$= 2n - 2$						$2n-2$											
18	+	$^1V_1 + ^2V_7$	$^3V_7$		$= 3 + 1 = 4$							4										
19	÷	$^4V_6 \div ^3V_7$	$^1V_9$		$= \dfrac{2n-2}{4}$									$\dfrac{2n-2}{4}$								
20	×	$^1V_9 \times ^3V_{11}$	$^4V_{11}$		$= \dfrac{2n}{2}\cdot\dfrac{2n-1}{3}\cdot\dfrac{2n-2}{4} = B_3 A_3$									0		$\left\{\dfrac{2n}{2}\,\dfrac{2n-1}{3}\,\dfrac{2n-2}{4}\right\} = A_3$						
21	×	$^2V_{22} \times ^4V_{11}$	$^2V_{12}$		$B_3 A_3$												$B_3 A_3$				B_3	
22	+	$^2V_{12} + ^2V_{13}$	$^3V_{13}$		$= A_0 + B_1 A_1 + B_3 A_3$												0	$\{A_0 + B_1 A_1 + B_3 A_3\}$				
23	−	$^3V_{10} - ^1V_1$	$^4V_{10}$		$= n - 3 (= 1)$										$n-3$							
					Here follows a repetition of Operations thirteen to twenty-three.						0	0			0		0					
24	+	$^4V_{13} \times ^0V_{24}$	$^1V_{24}$		$= B_7$																	B_7
25	+	$^1V_1 + ^1V_3$	$^1V_3$		$= n + 1 = 4 + 1 = 5$	1		$n+1$														

...by a Variable-card.
...by a Variable-card.

Note 'G'.

Above: The Difference
Engine.

Left: William King, Earl of
Lovelace, circa 1860.

velvet prison in the attic, it could now be displayed proudly on the wall. Along with the picture was an ink stand. In fairness to Lady Byron, she realised Ada was now in a position mentally to confront her father's past and with her husband there to support her through this process, it was perhaps an appropriate time for Ada to finally own her Byron roots. Now that she no longer bore that surname, it may have been an easier task to undertake. It was also after her marriage that she was finally allowed to read her father's poetry and to talk about it with others. Presumably William encouraged his wife to do this; he would have made an ideal partner to discuss and guide her on his works and may have been advised to direct his wife to certain works over others.

The marriage appeared to have got off to a good start, and Ada was pregnant during the Christmas of 1865. Their first child was born at 11 St James's Square, London on 12 May 1836. She had been safely delivered of a son. Lady Byron was given the honour of naming the baby and she surprisingly chose to name her first grandchild Byron, in honour of his grandfather; he was styled as Viscount Ockham. It was shortly after the birth of his son and heir on 30 June 1836 that the Prime Minister, Lord Melbourne, created William 1st Earl of Lovelace, making Ada the Countess of Lovelace. This was a title that had been created especially for William and his heirs. A baby girl followed on 22 September 1837, and she was called Anne Isabella, after her grandmother. A final child, another son, was born on 2 July 1839 and was called Ralph Gordon. The birth of Anne Isabella was difficult for Ada, and a bout of cholera quickly followed the birth, which resulted in her becoming very ill. Luckily the baby was not affected.

It was at this point that Ada became obsessed with her weight; she was concerned she had gained too much during her pregnancies and worryingly, she got to the point of starving herself in a bid to get her weight under control. This behaviour mimics that of her father, who was well-known for his battles with his fluctuating weight in his

71

younger years. Young Byron was Ada's favoured child, and she took great pleasure in applauding him. It took her a long time to grow close to her daughter; however, this may have been down to the illness after the birth and the lack of opportunity to bond with her. Baby Ralph was a firm favourite with his grandmother.

Ada was never overly maternal with any of her children. It was not a role that came naturally to her and she struggled to form any strong bonds but, to be fair, other than her grandmother, Lady Judith, she had not been in the presence of a loving maternal figure for much of her life. Ada tried her best with her children, but they were to become a source of worry and anxiety for her.

Following the births of the children, the marriage started to show cracks and in 1840, Ada and William started to slowly drift apart. This was partly due to their divided interests and his new role of Lord-Lieutenant of Surrey, which demanded much of his time. There was no grand explosion and separation was never discussed, but both must have realised that their marriage was struggling. After the birth of Ralph, Ada yearned for her freedom and a return to her studies. She turned to her old friend Babbage and asked him to recommend a tutor who could help get her mathematics learning back on track. Before long, she was in correspondence with Augustus de Morgan. He was a professor of mathematics at the University of London and he steered Ada through some complex mathematical equations. But Ada was struggling to find focus; with three young children and a husband to consider, she would get side-tracked and drift from one project to another. She even started to question the idea of imaginary numbers.

Ada was in a vulnerable state around this time, and this is borne out in her mental state regarding William and the state of their marriage. During a stay at Ashley Coombe, Ada visited her neighbour, the scientist Andrew Crosse, at his estate at Fyne Court, Broomfield, and it was here she met his son, John Crosse. He was to become Ada's assistant at Ockham and gossip soon started circulating that their relationship had developed into more than a professional one, which prompted Ada to start questioning her marriage. She had very conflicted ideas about her marriage, which sound rather like her father's thoughts on matrimony. One day, she regretted marrying William, and the next, she gushed over married life and claimed what a wonderful man he was and that he was the ideal man for her. Coupled with her differing opinions on her married life, Ada continued to remain detached from her children, which forced William to take a more active role in their upbringing. The children never had much affection for their father and the decision was made to separate them from each other in the hope it would be easier to manage them. All the children had a strong affection for their grandmother, and Ralph was put under the care of Lady Byron, whilst the elder two were put under the care of a governess called Miss Cooper.

After a while, Ada decided she wanted to take back control of Anne Isabella and her education, knowing how important her own education had been to her, so she appointed a new governess called Miss Wacheter, and she was put in charge of her welfare and teaching. The young girl thrived under her tutelage and the relationship between mother and daughter began to grow stronger.

Anne, as she became known, became fluent in many languages, including French, German, and Arabic and the latter would serve her well in later life when she travelled extensively through the Middle East. During one of her many trips, she became the first woman to ride through the Arabian desert to reach Ha'il in north-western Arabia. She was also a keen horsewoman and became heavily involved with the breeding of Arabian racehorses, along with her husband, the poet Wilfrid Blunt. Between them, they owned the Crabbet Arabian Stud in Surrey, England and the Sheykh Obeyd Estate near Cairo. They travelled widely during the late 1870s and early 1880s in search of the best purebred Arabian horses to import back to England to breed at Crabbet. The first six horses were bought in 1878 and the horses that were bred from those six changed the bloodstock of racehorses in the UK.

The Blunts were very successful and produced many winners and their horses have been sold all over the world. They may have experienced great success with the stud farm but sadly, their marriage was not as successful and was very unhappy; it did, however, produce one surviving child, a daughter called Judith, who would later become 16th Baroness Wentworth. Anne had previously inherited the title shortly before she died in 1917, following the death of her niece Ada King-Milbanke, daughter of Ralph and his first wife. After enduring many of her husband's extramarital affairs, Anne finally reached breaking point in 1906 and left Wilfrid. Like her grandmother before her, she saw no way out of her troubled married life other than separation – both had a young daughter to consider. When the couple formally separated, Anne was permitted to keep the Crabbet stud and half of its livestock. She spent her remaining years at her estate in Egypt, where she died on 15 December 1917. She left the running of the Crabbet Estate to Judith and her husband.

But what of the other Lovelace children? The young Lord Ockham was sent to sea at just 13 years old and didn't return until the age of 16. He sailed on the *Swift* to Tasmania and managed to rise to the rank of officer, but he later deserted and worked his passage back to Britain and became a shipyard worker in London. He inherited the Wentworth barony following the death of Lady Byron but sadly died just two years later, unmarried, at the young age of 26. He also championed the poor against the rich in much the same way his grandparents had. Ockham was thought to be the most like his grandfather – he was physically attractive, charming, and made friends easily. He also had the rebellious Byron streak and was never one to be forced to do something against his will. The worry was that he had inherited a little too much of his grandfather's traits and, in order to safeguard from any potential scandal, the decision was made to keep him away from his younger sister in case he developed a sexual interest in her. Despite showing none of the Byron badness, Ralph was also separated from her, and the siblings were never allowed to be left alone together.

The Lovelace children were starting to become a cause for concern for their parents; they displayed unruly behaviour and were fast becoming uncontrollable. Their German tutor had failed in his attempts at correcting their wild ways and Ada was unwilling to step in or allow William to do the same, so he turned to Lady Byron to ask her for guidance. She felt the children needed someone new to teach them, someone who could set them new boundaries and hopefully put them on the path to better behaviour. Luckily, she found a Bristol-born teacher called Dr William Carpenter who was willing to join the household to teach the children. But Lady Byron, being Lady Byron, would not just have hired anyone, she wanted someone who could not only keep track of the children but also someone who was capable of keeping tabs on Ada too. Lady Byron was concerned by her daughter's recent behaviour and wanted to know what she was up to and if there was anything to be worried about. Carpenter was hired to see if he could come up with a solution to Ada's behaviour, so, without William's knowledge, he was sent to spy on her and report back directly to Lady Byron.

This was a highly covert operation between the two of them and he knew he could make some serious demands of Lady Byron in return for his information and discretion; his list of requests included, rather boldly, a house of his own and the freedom to travel to London whenever he desired to attend and give lectures. Lady Byron agreed and soon he was installed as the children's new tutor. Being in such close contact with Ada meant he managed to build up a relationship of trust with her and he found her to be frustrated and thwarted. She felt she was being held back from pursuing her scientific works, due to her commitments as a wife and mother, which probably increased her resentment of both.

Carpenter also found her physical wellbeing to be suffering too; she had a stomach complaint that was causing her some discomfort, which in turn was leading to bouts of depression. Her mental health was now a growing cause for concern too and that needed to be addressed immediately lest she plummet into a deep depressive state. In his progress report to Lady Byron, he claimed it would be in Ada's best interests if she was given the time to discuss and focus on her emotional self and, in order to help with this, he offered to be her emotional outlet. He made the suggestion that she wrote to him, baring her soul, telling him all her worries and concerns. He convinced her that letting all her pent-up feelings out on the page would help her come to terms with her emotions and to process them to reach an understanding with herself.

In her letters, Ada declared she felt detached from her loved ones and, after years of study, she felt distance between herself and her feelings. It is almost like she had become a machine and was incapable of emotion; the after effects of an emotionless childhood, would appear to have caused Ada to forget how to love, or she had never actually learnt how to express her feelings and now, as an adult, she was struggling to process them. Even more worrying for her family was the revelation that she had been having suicidal thoughts and she confessed that she had come close to poisoning herself.

It would appear that at this time in her life, Ada was in a desperately sad situation, desperate for someone or something to rescue her from a looming abyss that threatened to consume her. Were these feelings down to genetics? Maybe the Byron curse was finally taking hold, or perhaps it was a hangover from a childhood that showed her very little affection and love. For all Lady Byron's harsh parenting stance in Ada's childhood, it would appear the adult was becoming everything she had fought against, but the irony was that her harsh, cold mothering style had damaged Ada so much that it pushed her towards the mental fragility she was so frightened of. Nature and nurture appeared to battle against each other for all of Ada's life – after being consistently told not to be something, it looked like she had no control over who she naturally was. Lady Byron could only have done so much in protecting her daughter against such demons, but if it was in her nature, then that battle would never truly be won.

As Ada got older and became a wife and mother, it appeared that her Byron blood was winning the war. She had now reached a point in her life when her actions had impacts on others; she had responsibilities beyond just herself and that pressure was proving too much for her to cope with. Carpenter tried to reassure Ada that she needn't be concerned and that what she was experiencing was natural. He told her that he would help nurture her feelings and come to terms with her complicated emotions, and soon correspondence between the two was becoming very frequent. By this time, Ada was desperate for some emotional attention; with William often away, she was lacking an emotional crutch she could lean against, so when Carpenter made this suggestion, she readily poured out her feelings and allowed him into her confidence. When William was at home, their relationship was cordial and respectful, but in terms of emotion, by this stage, it seems there was very little of it. Carpenter, on the other hand, was more than willing to show her some emotion and offered her an outlet for all the pent-up anguish she was feeling.

What Ada really needed was a brotherly figure who could look out for her without any form of romantic attachment, someone who had her best interests at heart but with no other obligation on her part. Unfortunately, Carpenter had other ideas, and soon there was more trouble attaching itself to Ada. Either he had misunderstood her intentions or saw an opportunity to take full advantage of her vulnerable emotional state, but he made a pass at her and kissed her, to which she took great offence. She was quick to put Carpenter in his place and this was followed by a swift rebuff from her husband. She had made the error of telling him and Lady Byron what had been happening, assuming they would be understanding. Her mother was disappointed in her, which seems a tad unfair, considering it was at her suggestion that Carpenter had integrated himself with Ada. William was naturally livid, not just that his wife had entered into a correspondence of this nature behind his back, but that she had been so naïve as to put herself in this compromising position in the first place.

Carpenter, on the other hand, did not know when to leave well enough alone and goaded William. He decided his best response would be to retaliate and went on to make the bold claim that if the marriage had been in better shape, then Ada would not have needed to seek comfort from another man. Unable to stop there, he took this a step further and even accused Ada of being the one who instigated the whole thing. He insisted that she had led him on, despite it being him that encouraged her to open up to him. He also accused her of being an unfeeling wife; this seems like an unfair accusation to make against her, for she may not have been in love with William, but she would not have behaved in a way that would have caused him upset and hurt.

It all sounds like sour grapes on Carpenter's behalf. Perhaps he was unhappy at the fact his advances had not been reciprocated as he would have hoped; after all, he knew Ada was vulnerable and a Byron – her supposed loose morals should have made her an easy target with men like him. Carpenter did not come out of this scandal too badly and was paid £300 to leave the employ of the Lovelaces, which, considering this amount equalled Ada's annual allowance, can be considered a substantial amount. Despite her anger at him for taking advantage of her good nature, Ada was sad to see him leave; once again, she was feeling trapped and emotionally stunted and, thanks to Carpenter's actions, she no longer had anyone to turn to for support. She had finally confessed to herself that she did not love William in the way a wife perhaps ought to, but she did care for him. There may have been no love on her part but she did respect him. For William's part, he had helped his wife in the best way he could and would always be there to support her, but how he felt when he realised her true feelings we can only speculate. He may even have known all along that his wife was not in love with him, but he remained loyal to Ada and the marriage survived this indiscretion.

Ada had never really had a strong male figure in her life since perhaps her grandfather, Ralph. Her mother had never remarried and she had no uncles that she could turn to, so it is interesting to speculate whether she was perhaps looking for a father figure in William, rather than a husband. He was older than her, but that was not unusual in Victorian times. He was handsome enough but Ada was a passionate woman; maybe physically she felt William lacked in that department, so, she felt more of a paternal love rather than a physical love. That said, they had three children earlier on in their marriage, but as they got older, she may have felt the age difference more keenly. William was wealthy and could offer her that male protection she yearned for, he was safe and reliable and she knew he would protect her, just as any father would.

Perhaps, when she married William, Ada felt that he would be the kind of man she could desire long term. But as time went on, something in the Lovelace marriage changed and that change came from Ada herself. It was also during this time that she started to seriously question her role as a mother and her suitability at looking after her own children. She often found them tiresome and felt she had no positive impact on their lives, with nothing to offer them either emotionally or practically. How she could offer them emotional support when she struggled so much herself is a difficult thing for any mother to come to terms with; instead, it became another stick that she used to beat herself with.

It is hardly surprising that Ada felt like this, considering her own relationship with her parents – she did not exactly have good role models when it came to being a good parent and, even at this stage, it seemed unlikely that she could turn to Lady Byron for support or advice. She could not be described as having a normal functioning parental style, and she was far from the ideal role model for Ada to look to when she herself was a new mother. Surely it can be no coincidence that both women struggled to bond with their children and that the feelings of confusion and an overwhelming sense of inadequacy Ada experienced were not too dissimilar from those of her father. As well as dealing with her emotional fragility, Ada's physical health was continuing to cause her some concern and, in order to get this under control, she started to develop an ever-increasing dependence on alcohol and drugs such as laudanum. The administering of opium was encouraged by Dr Locock, who advised that taking the drug every few days would help ease her discomfort, provided she stayed away from anything that could cause her any undue excitement on those days.

Taking into consideration all the challenges the Lovelaces faced, it was inevitable that as time went on, they would continue to drift further and further apart. Soon they found themselves so emotionally detached from one another that they began to lead independent lives. Both were absorbed in their own activities; Ada had her scientific work and William was occupied with his many posts and projects, including the renovations and expansion of Horsley Towers, an estate bought by William in Surrey. His plans included the building of a great hall, chapel, and work room for Ada, although she did not enjoy spending time there. There were many factors that caused the marriage to falter, not least the couple themselves; they were very different people and whilst William was aware that his wife was liable to ill health and emotional problems, they continued to rub along together. Their marriage may have been under long term strain but, as time would tell, William would be there to support his wife through her difficult times. He would always aim to do his best by Ada, and he would also lend his support when Ada was confronted with her father's past. Now she was an adult; it was time she learnt the full extent of his behaviour.

William and Ada travelled to Paris in 1841 to meet Medora Leigh, daughter of Augusta and supposedly Lord Byron. He had alluded to this during one of his mental breakdowns, shortly after his marriage. It would appear that Medora was in trouble in France and had turned to Lady Byron for help. She had already travelled to Paris in the hope of providing some assistance to Medora. As she had with her own daughter, Lady Byron saw this as an opportunity to gain a certain level of control over Medora and at the same time saw it as a chance to enact revenge on her mother by revealing that she was the product of an incestuous relationship and that Lord Byron was her father.

It would appear that Medora had been set up by her jealous sister, Georgiana. She was seduced by her sister's husband, Henry Trevanion, and quickly fell pregnant; she gave birth prematurely in Calais and then returned home to continue living with her unassuming mother in London. What happened to the child is unclear, although, given it was born early, it more than likely died shortly after the birth. Medora fell pregnant for a second time by Henry during a visit to Augusta's. When her father, Colonel Leigh, heard of this, he flew into a rage and demanded Medora return from Bath immediately, where she had been staying with the Trevanion family. When she returned home, her father placed her under house arrest whilst he decided the best course of action. Being unmarried and pregnant was a scandal but being unmarried and pregnant by your sister's husband was something else entirely. The family may have been used to the odd family scandal in the past, but it seems this time it was a step too far.

Henry and Georgiana managed to track Medora down and he made the bold decision to leave Georgiana and their three children behind to elope to northern France with Medora, where they lived under assumed names. What Georgiana thought of this we can only imagine; it would seem her earlier plot to discredit her sister had backfired on her, and now she found herself abandoned with a young family to support. Medora gave birth to a healthy girl in May 1834; she called her Marie. By the time 1838 came around, Henry had a new mistress and Medora and her child were surplus to requirements. He seemed to think nothing of abandoning women with children in pursuit of his own enjoyment. Medora fell ill soon after but managed to write to her mother – she needed a deed from her that would help her claim £3,000, but Augusta refused, and Medora turned to Lady Byron for help.

It was at this time that Lady Byron finally revealed to Ada that she believed Byron was Medora's father. Ada was not surprised by this revelation and confessed to her mother that she had often felt embarrassed at the thoughts she had regarding Medora's parentage and had long thought them sisters. Lady Byron claimed she had never done anything to make Ada think this, but she must have heard some gossip in order to come to that conclusion. Had William perhaps unwittingly said something to his wife that had planted the thought in her mind? Regardless of how she came to believe this, it did give mother and daughter an opportunity to finally open up and talk about Ada's father in a way that had so far been impossible. It might have helped Ada if this conversation had happened earlier, but nonetheless, she was about to learn all there was to know, albeit from Lady Byron's point of view. Ada naturally wanted to know as much as she could about her parents' marriage, how they met, and the true reasons behind their split. Lady Byron told her all about the relationship between Augusta and her father and initially Ada was outraged, but she soon changed her mind and decided her father's reputation needed saving and she was going to be the one to do it. She claimed, 'I have an ambition to make a compensation to mankind for his misused genius! If he has transmitted to me any portion of that genius, I would use it to bring out great truths and principles. I think he has bequeathed this task to me!'

It is touching that Ada felt compelled to defend a father she had never known, regardless of the charges laid before him. It felt like the world was against him and it was her duty as his daughter to help mend his tarnished reputation. It is important to note that now she was married, she had someone else's opinion of him; all her childhood, she had heard negative comments regarding her father and his behaviour, but now William was on hand to give Ada an alternative viewpoint. We know he was an admirer of Lord Byron so he may have softened the stories and offered a more neutral version of events.

Ada and Medora first met in Paris in April 1841 at the request of Lady Byron. Initially Ada showed a sisterly interest in her; she was friendly and polite and was willing to welcome Medora into her family, but Lady Byron had other ideas and was up to her old tricks again. She began manipulating the situation by trying to convince Ada of Medora's terrible past. Ada was aware of her past and was still willing to overlook that and see this meeting as an opportunity to mend old wounds and move forward together. Lady Byron was taking a very keen interest in Medora, which is strange considering she thought her to be the product of an incestuous affair which had contributed to her marital breakdown, but the careful and considerate treatment of Medora was not by accident. Lady Byron was never a woman who did anything on a whim – all her decisions were carefully thought through before she committed herself to them. The purpose of this latest act was her way of exacting revenge against Augusta. Soon enough, they all returned to England and Lady Byron set about using Medora to prove that she was right to leave Byron. Again, she was constantly looking for a reason to vindicate her earlier life decisions; she could not let the issue lie and in Medora she finally had the vital piece of evidence to confirm her former husband's misdeeds.

Lady Byron saw Medora as hardened proof that she had been justified in her decision to leave her husband and Medora's anger and resentment towards her mother helped back this up. It was also an opportunity to show how kind and considerate she was, looking after the child of that unlawful union – how caring Lady Byron was to step in and assist the young woman at her time of need. But soon enough, when Medora was not getting what she wanted, namely the deed and money, she started lashing out at the people around her, including Lady Byron. This alerted Ada to the possibility that all was not as it should be and that something was going on that she did not know about. In the end, Lady Byron paid for Medora to return to France, but that did not put an end to her constant hounding. Medora begged her to send money across the channel so that she could fund her French lifestyle; she enjoyed staying in the best hotels and expected Lady Byron to foot the bill. She thought Medora was mad but just like Byron, she could not prove it.

As far as Ada was concerned, she took offence to the way Medora was treating her mother. She thought her ungrateful and so she cut all ties with her in 1844. Medora died from smallpox in 1849. The parallels between Ada and Medora are very interesting. If we assume that Medora was indeed the natural daughter of Lord Byron, then the differences between the two are stark. Ada, whilst she was liable to the odd bit of scandal, was never morally bankrupt, unlike Medora, who had numerous affairs, including one with her brother-in-law. She was open to bribery, begged for money, and lived well beyond her means. It is quite possible Ada would have turned out like this had Lady Byron not stepped in and ruled over her with an iron fist. Maybe that strict upbringing was beneficial after all.

Sadly, many scandals seemed to attach themselves to Ada. Her Byron name still ensured she remained a source of public interest. Was Ada an easy target for men? Did they assume that because she was Byron's daughter, she was fair game and morally bankrupt and would be easily seduced from her marital obligations? Carpenter certainly thought she was; whether he had any genuine feelings for her or not we cannot be certain, but what we do know is that he took advantage of a woman who had been lured into a vulnerable situation and encouraged, by him, to lay her soul bare.

When it comes to men, Ada does come across as being incredibly naïve; she readily believed that this man was concerned for nothing more than her emotional wellbeing, but from his point of view, Ada was there to be taken advantage of. He may very well have had strong feelings for her and wanted to develop a relationship, but that does seem unlikely, given the way he reacted once his actions had been discovered. His pride had certainly been dented and his character was not redeemed when he made further demands on the family. He had them all worked out from the first day of his employment and we cannot be sure when he formed the plan to try to seduce Ada. He appears to have manipulated the situation for his own gain from day one. It is surprising that Lady Byron had been fooled into employing him in the first place – knowing her daughter's emotional state, it does seem unusual that she would encourage or indeed allow a man to have such close access to Ada, and the idea of keeping this from her husband is very questionable behaviour. The quick and decisive action taken by William and his mother-in-law potentially saved Ada from huge embarrassment and scandal. It is hard to imagine her reputation recovering from the taint of an extramarital affair, as up until that point, the Lovelace marriage had been a true love match to those on the outside. Even William had thought his marriage was sound.

At this stage in her life, Ada appeared to be lost. She was unfulfilled in her personal life as well as being frustrated in her studies, she felt inadequate as a wife and mother and felt trapped. Now that her one supposed friend had turned out to be a fraud, Ada's isolation grew, but as always, controversy was never too far away. To help with her hysteria, Ada developed a passion for music and drama; she even took up singing lessons in a bid to soothe her mind. She also developed a worrying love of poetry but felt the novel was not worthy of being classed as a book. Her behaviour was becoming more and more unpredictable, her style of dress was unconventional, and she had the ability to cause a stir at any dinner party. Her topics of conversation were often questionable, and many put this down to her use of laudanum and claret.

In September 1850, Ada and William went on a trip to discover more about her famous father and her Byron roots. She made the decision that the time had come to finally learn who her father and ancestors were, where they lived, and to know where she fitted into their story. Ada was now at a point in her life in which she needed to gain a sense of her true identity. Was she a true Byron or had her mother succeeded in removing any trace of her father and his family? There was only one place she would find these answers and so their first stop on a tour of the Midlands and Yorkshire was Nottinghamshire and the true home of the Byron family.

Chapter Five

Gambling

On 7 September 1850, Ada made her first and only visit to her ancestral home of Newstead Abbey. Accompanied by William and free from Lady Byron's influence, she hoped that by visiting the former country seat of her father, she would be able to build up her own image of him in her mind. The Abbey dated back to the Middle Ages, when a monastic house was founded by King Henry II in 1163. It later became a ruin at the time of the dissolution of the monasteries, during the reign of Henry VIII in 1539. Just a year later, he granted the property to John Byron of Colwick and he set about turning the old priory into a family home.

The Abbey had gone through a lot of changes between then and the poet Byron's ownership. The land and estate had suffered at the hands of the 'Wicked Lord' due to his own money issues, which saw many of Newstead Abbey's treasures sold, so when Byron assumed the title in 1798, it was very much a shadow of its former glory. Lord Byron had not lived at Newstead Abbey since 1814, and when he entered his self-imposed exile, it became necessary for him to sell the property. He struggled to find a buyer but eventually his friend Colonel Thomas Wildman bought it for £94,500 in 1818. Wildman had the money to restore Newstead Abbey to its former glory and he was faithful in keeping to the medieval heritage of the building. He wanted to keep the character and he ensured the Norman and gothic styles were preserved. The work had been completed by the time of the Lovelaces' visit, and Ada and William's lodgings overlooked the gothic fountain and the grounds beyond.

On first impression, Ada thought Newstead Abbey was a dark and depressing place, which left her feeling subdued and withdrawn with a sadness that it was no longer a Byron home. It is an atmospheric building and when surrounded with the history of her family, it is no wonder she began to feel a sense of attachment to it – she belonged there. The Byron spirit seems to live within the walls of Newstead Abbey and any visitor there today cannot fail to come away with a sense of Lord Byron being present. He seems to stalk the corridors. For Ada, it would have been the closest she had ever felt to her father. The corridors and rooms are dark, and the haunting feel of the Abbey dominates the senses; it is gothic in the truest meaning of the word. Despite a faltering start, the visit seemed to awaken something deep inside Ada, and her emotions were soon aware of a sense of loss. Whether that was a material loss that this great residence was no longer part of her family, or if it was a familial loss of never having the opportunity to know her father, we cannot be sure, but the fact that up until this point she was never able to make a true connection with him must have been overwhelming when she came into contact with his home, for there is no escaping the shroud of Byron that hangs over it.

When Ada took delivery of the Albanian portrait, it would have brought him into her home and into her conscience; finally, she could put a face to a name and to a certain extent, you can gauge a person's character from a picture. She may have seen something within his eyes that she herself could relate to. But to walk in the footsteps of that person brings them to life; his surroundings and belongings all of a sudden become tangible. She could look out over the same views he did and touch items he had touched. Perhaps the brooding nature of Newstead Abbey finally fully awoke her Byron blood.

It is important that we do not underestimate the role of Newstead Abbey when we build a picture of Byron and his life – the gothic surroundings of the Abbey live and breathe through his poems, and the ruined nature of the old Abbey is reflected in the ruin of Byron's life. The crumbling edifice of the old cloisters and the ruin of the ancient western front all symbolise the ruin of this once great noble family. Three days into the visit, Ada confessed to Wildman that she felt sadness and loss when she walked the rooms and grounds. He was a friend of Byron's and would have wanted her to feel a true connection to him and his home, so he began telling her of him, which led her to becoming absorbed with her surroundings and reaching out to connect to her Byronic roots.

The time had finally come for Ada to get to know her father. She wanted to hear all there was to know about him, good or bad. She was prepared for what he was about to say, she had already heard certain stories, but now she wanted to know it all through Wildman and he was more than happy to oblige, and patiently answered any questions she had. Listening carefully to his replies, she may have finally realised she was her father's daughter. Perhaps she picked out certain character traits that she saw in herself from Wildman's description and finally felt that connection to her past that she had waited so long for, confirmation that she belonged.

Having never met him and having grown up in the strict care of her mother, Ada was able to fantasise about what kind of father Byron would have made. No doubt he would have shown Ada love and tenderness that had so lacked in Lady Byron; she had provided Ada with the kind of education she had enjoyed and both women were more than adept at mathematics and logic, but it feels like there was always another side to Ada's personality that she couldn't quite understand. But after her visit to Newstead Abbey, the pieces were slotting into place for her – answers to the questions she had waited so long for, explanations as to why she felt and did the things she did were now becoming clearer to her. She knew there was something about her father that she was being protected from and she had spent so much of her life questioning herself, her mindset, and her actions that she seemed to be, at times, anguished by her morality. But finally coming to Newstead Abbey provided her with those answers she had craved for so long. Ada was a Byron. There was no escaping that fact, no matter how much her mother had tried to banish him from her daughter's life. No matter what his faults were, that could never be altered. The time had come for Ada to acknowledge she was a Byron and had she known more of her father from an earlier age, she might have had a clearer sense of who she was. It could have saved her years of anguish. But now she did feel that connection to her Byron ancestors and she was going to fully embrace it, much to her mother's disappointment.

The news that Ada had developed an admiration for her father and Newstead Abbey was not what Lady Byron had wanted to hear. In Lady Byron's mind, Ada's acceptance of her father must mean that she thought her mother was at fault for the breakdown of their marriage. Clearly this is not true; Lady Byron's reason for leaving was and always has been justified, but her obsession with Byron meant the issue could never be left alone. She now felt accused by Ada, like she was calling into question why she had abandoned Byron at a vulnerable time for him, when in fact, in her mind, she had saved him by leaving. Lady Byron took the perceived slight a step too far and threatened Ada, stating that she would have no more to do with her grandchildren if they were being brought up to believe their grandmother guilty of such cold and callous behaviour. Naturally, Ada responded with denials, claiming she had been fed no information that put her mother in a negative light from Wildman, but that did not seem to win Lady Byron over.

She quite clearly overreacted to this whole affair. Byron was long dead and posed no threat to her. Ada was now an adult and capable of understanding and coming to her own conclusions regarding her parents' marriage and subsequent split, without the need for her mother to contribute to her own thoughts. But Lady Byron felt that after all the hard work she had put in since the separation, it was hard to stomach the admiration from Ada; in her eyes, her father could now do no wrong. Knowing what we do of Lady Byron's character, it was an understandable reaction from her. She was hurting and it stung; however, you cannot help but think all this heartache and anguish could have been avoided for both women if she had only explained to Ada, when she was at an appropriate age, the full details of the marriage and separation – then she would have been able to determine herself who was in the right or wrong. Shrouding everything to do with her father in mystery only worked to make him untouchable later on.

After all, Ada was a married woman herself and fully appreciated how difficult married life could be. She had had her fair share of problems with William and, armed with all the facts, she could have come to a conclusion all of her own and not cast blame when there was none to be had. It is as though Lady Byron never trusted her daughter with the full knowledge, worried, perhaps, that it would lead to more and more questions and that Ada would misinterpret the finer details and side with her father. But this was not about taking sides – too much time had passed for that. All Ada wanted, and in truth what she was entitled too, was honesty from her mother. Lady Byron's constant coercive control of Ada had now got to the point where she was fighting back. She was a married woman with children of her own and had finally realised she did not need to bend to her mother's will. She had no need to adhere to her rules on how she ought to live her life any longer.

The threats Lady Byron made to boycott caring for her grandchildren were nothing short of manipulative behaviour. She loved her grandchildren and to use them in an attempt to once again put a wedge between Ada and her father was spiteful and damaging. She does not seem to have taken into consideration the impact this would have had on them; they adored their grandmother and she knew this, which makes the threat all the crueller. It appears that Lady Byron was the only person who was allowed to be obsessed with Byron. She wanted the monopoly on the hurt and the grief he had caused, she was the martyr, and that was all there was to it in her mind.

All Ada wanted was to understand where she came from; she harboured no obsessive desire to become him or be like him – that was down to nature and she was tired of fighting against it. The time had finally come for Ada to defend herself and her name against her mother. If she did not like it, that was Lady Byron's issue, not Ada's. This whole episode awoke something in Ada. The scales started to fall from her eyes, and she finally freed herself from her mother's vice-like grip. She decided she was no longer going to suffer under her mother's influence, and she was finally free to live her life as she deemed appropriate. William, it appears, supported his wife in this, although he was well aware that leaving Ada to her own devices opened her up to be taken advantage of.

Ada's newfound freedom worried Lady Byron, and she had to find a way to regain control over her daughter. She backtracked on her original threats and made a grand gesture by offering to buy Newstead Abbey for the Lovelaces, but after an initial valuation, the matter is never mentioned again. Ada claimed, 'I do love the venerable old place and all my wicked forefathers.' She had obviously made a connection there, which proved she was far more Byron than Milbanke, and that was a fact she was now happy to acknowledge. Unfortunately for Ada, her newly appreciated Byron genes were going to haunt her a lot quicker than she could have anticipated. She would not need to try hard to show the world she was her father's daughter.

The couple's tour continued, and Ada went to stay at Aske Hall, home of the 2nd Earl of Zetland and his family, whilst William attended to business elsewhere, including a trip to Lincolnshire to investigate new agricultural methods that had piqued his interest. Ada decided this was not the kind of trip she would enjoy so she stayed behind. The Zetland family owned the 1850 Derby and St Leger Stakes winner Voltigeur, and whilst she was their guest, they took Ada to the races at Doncaster. Ada had always had a keen interest in the horses, and it was at Doncaster that she made the fateful decision that gambling on the horses would be the best way to recoup some of the Lovelace fortune and try to amass some funds for the building of the Analytical Engine. She felt she could calculate the mathematical equations that could outwit the bookmakers; all she needed was a syndicate of wealthy friends to place the bets for her. She was backed by a Dr Malcolm, who was Zetland's own physician and who had briefly treated Ada during her stay with the family.

Buoyed by this idea, Ada began to grow her trusted circle and started to study the form. By January 1851, she had set up her gambling group, consisting of John Crosse, William Nightingale, Mr Fleming, the very wealthy Richard Ford, and Dr Malcolm. Babbage knew of her plans but did not appear to contribute financially; if he thought the idea an absurd one, he did not say so and did little to discourage his friends from getting involved. How much William knew about her plans at this stage is unclear, but he must have had an inkling as to what was going on, as he knew the fellow members and had noticed Ada's newfound love of horse racing and placing bets. The syndicate made it through one full racing season, so it can be assumed they had a modicum of success and made some money, so they decided to carry on to a much more ambitious plan.

On 1 May 1851, there was a showdown between The Flying Dutchman, an English thoroughbred, and Voltigeur, as the pair went head-to-head at York in what was billed as 'The Great Match'. It was to be The Flying Dutchman's last race and, as it turned out, it was a disaster for Ada and her syndicate, as Voltigeur lost, and as a result they suffered heavy losses. Ada quite clearly was not to be put off by this loss, and she somehow managed to persuade William to lend Dr Malcolm £1,800 to bet against Teddington in the 1851 Derby. Unfortunately, Teddington won by two lengths, and the losses incurred were mammoth. Whether it was bad luck or bad knowledge, we do not know, but the syndicate did not seem very good at backing a winner. But where did the fault lie – was it with Ada and her calculations, or the syndicate, who were supposedly studying the form?

Ada had always had passion for horses and racing, but she developed a more serious interest in the late 1840s, and by the early 1850s, her enthusiasm was so great that she told her mother all about her plans. Naturally Lady Byron disapproved, as gambling was seen as immoral and therefore a Byronic trait – it had, after all, ruined her forefathers – but to be fair to her, any mother would do their best to try to dissuade their child from becoming embroiled in such a wild fantasy as this; it was clear to any outsider that this was a scheme that was doomed for failure.

As time went on, the gambling became a serious concern for Ada. She had fallen into the trap of upping her stakes to cover the ever-increasing losses, which she could ill afford, and by 1850, she was in debt to the tune of £500, approximately £40,000 in today's money. When we bear in mind her annual allowance from William was just £300, we can appreciate the true cost of her losses and what that meant for Ada. She had no option but to try to recoup some of the losses by borrowing some of the money from her mother and to make personal sacrifices such as dismissing her lady's maid and tightening her belt in terms of her domestic costs. Despite borrowing from them, she was desperate to keep the true costs of her losses from William and her mother. They knew she had debts but had no idea how serious they were – had they known, they perhaps would have stepped in to prevent this from going any further, but they had no inkling, and the debts escalated even more. Ada was a highly intelligent woman with a mathematical brain to rival the greatest men of the day, but sadly she rarely backed a winner. She may have thought she had nailed the mathematical calculations, but she lacked knowledge of the sport.

It was time to up the ante. Ada wanted to put her talents to use, and she thought that if she could apply mathematical principles to her gambling and her new set of friends could provide her with a syndicate to raise enough funds, she could provide the scientific formula to help predict the odds. On paper, it sounds like a great idea, but Ada, and her syndicate to a certain degree, were naïve to think they could beat the system. She thought she had come up with a fool-proof guarantee to win at the races. The men in the circle were not so sure but did little to discourage her; after all, on the off chance she was successful, then the winnings could be substantial. Ada's ambitious plan would mean she would take on the role of the bookmaker rather than being the person placing the bets. As a woman, she needed William's approval to take part in any scheme where gambling was involved, and given her past failures and losses, he would have been forgiven for declining, but Ada obviously held sway over her husband and he granted her his written permission to place bets, providing she was sensible. This was rather naïve on William's part, and soon enough, it would be a decision that would cost him thousands of pounds. All she had to do now was reassure her group that the calculations were sound and the bets could be placed. This was a high-risk grand scale operation. Ada sent men to visit different racecourses to study the form and based on information they fed back to her, she would then place bets within the syndicate, and from there, she would then use those funds to place her own bets with other bookmakers. This was an incredibly dangerous strategy and it turned out to be utterly disastrous.

Ada had once again backed the wrong horses, but this time the total losses reached a staggering £3,200, approximately £250,000 in today's money. The syndicate were understandably angry and were soon blackmailing Ada in an attempt to regain their losses. With no one to confide in, she had to turn once again to dependable William for help. He very generously settled the outstanding debt, but only on the agreement that the role Ada played was never to be revealed to the wider world – her honour must not be damaged by this. So, once again, deals were being made in an attempt to protect Ada and her fragile reputation and, like the earlier instances, it was never bad behaviour that threatened to bring Ada down but more her bad judgement and naivety. She seemed to have an unfortunate knack of putting herself in tricky situations and trusting others to the point that she was taken advantage of; we saw it with Carpenter and we see it again here. She was too willing to think the best of people and each time, she got her fingers burnt.

Ada's gambling was a sure sign that there was something of Byron about her, but it also shows her naivety in that she felt she actually could produce a mathematical formula that could outwit the bookmakers. She seems to have ignored the fact that there are events that would be beyond her control. For example, would the horse fall? Would the jockey be unseated? What were the course and weather conditions like? All this Ada had absolutely no way of knowing or predicting, so she could only ever have based her calculations on past form and the chance that none of these factors would come into play, but even then, a result was in no way guaranteed.

I find it hard to understand why someone as well-educated as Ada did not take these factors into consideration; the element of luck is needed in any sport and you can never beat the system, for you can never predict the future. I also find it surprising that the fellow syndicate members agreed to plough so much money into a scheme that appeared to be doomed from the start; these were well-educated wealthy men, who really should have known better than to get involved in such a wild scheme. Perhaps Ada's charm won them over, but by allowing her to continue with this plan, they unwittingly set her up to fail on a massive scale.

Ada's intentions in setting up this syndicate were, of course, well placed – this was not a 'get rich quick' scheme for her own greed, she had no grand desires to lavishly furnish her home or buy priceless pieces of art, she just wanted to contribute something to someone. She wanted to help replenish the depleted Lovelace fortunes, which were ironically now in a worse state due to her debts, but she also wanted to gain enough money to help Babbage build the Analytical Engine. At this stage, Babbage had still not managed to achieve any funding for his engine, and Ada wanted to get it built for her own ends. She had been desperate to reengage with her studies, and if she could help get the engine built, then it might have meant she could work further towards understanding and perhaps enhancing its capabilities. She could have developed her thoughts and ideas, which would have meant the Engine could have flourished far beyond what it was originally built to do.

Had she been given the opportunity to advance her studies and work, her health might have held out that bit longer, but sadly, the gambling fiasco had an adverse effect on Ada, and soon her worries would be compounded by her ever-failing health. For someone with a mind so strong and active, her physical body was weak and feeble in comparison, and soon she was going to find herself unable to help Babbage, or anyone else for that matter, any further. This must have been an incredibly frustrating time for Ada. Knowing that her mind was still capable of great things but finding herself physically unable to act on those thoughts and feelings must have left her angry with herself and her increasingly limited physical frailties.

William proved to be a dependable husband throughout Ada's gambling troubles; by giving his written permission, he implicated himself in the whole saga and therefore put himself in a position that left him liable for Ada's substantial losses. He may have hoped she could have controlled herself better and known when to stop the scheme, but he trusted her and that was an expensive mistake to make. You cannot help but wonder why Ada did not try to raise the money to build the Analytical Engine via other means. After all, she was well-connected to men and families of wealth, including her own mother, so what stopped her from turning to one of them and saving herself from the burden of attempting to raise the funds by herself?

We can speculate on why she chose this option. At this time, the relationship with her mother was strained, so it was unlikely she would turn in that direction for financial assistance, and as far as William is concerned, he may not have had the level of wealth that would help – instead he made himself useful by paying Ada's debts. But we must also look at the option that Ada was addicted to gambling. She had an addictive nature, as she had proven with her dependence on laudanum, so it could merely have come down to the thrill of the chase and the buzz of winning big.

People have often speculated on what Ada wanted the money for. It is believable that she wanted to help Babbage to get the Analytical

Engine built; she knew how much it would benefit society as a whole if it could be lifted from the drawings and made a reality. Others thought the plan was to recuperate the Lovelace fortunes, but how they had suffered so much loss is not quite clear. William had received a substantial dowry from his marriage to Ada and, other than the re-modelling and renovation of Horsley Towers, it is not clear where the other money had gone. Whatever the reason, it ended in complete disaster and from this point on, Ada's health began to rapidly deteriorate.

The horse racing furore turned out to be Ada's last foray in public life. It was to be a sad end to such a vibrant life and from here on in, she quickly fell victim to her final illness. She entered her sick chamber, never to recover from the ailments that now left her in constant agony that racked her body. The gambling woes added much strain to Ada mentally and her already fragile physical state could no longer sustain the ongoing ravages that she was experiencing day in day out. The pain had now become too much for her to endure and after being knocked down by the failure to succeed at the horses, Ada could no longer fight against her body.

Chapter Six

Death

By 1851, Ada was in very poor health. She had always suffered from ill health – even when she was a young child, she had always suffered some ailment or another, which would cause her to undertake periods of convalescence, but by this stage in her life, it had become serious and could no longer be overlooked. Both Dr Lee and the physician Sir James Clark examined Ada and diagnosed her with suffering from cancer of the womb, otherwise known as uterine cancer. Dr Locock undertook the physical examination of Ada and discovered her cervix was riddled with tumours.

Once told of this devastating news, William decided that it would be best for his wife if she was not told the full extent of her illness, as it would cause her even more unnecessary stress. Whether she had an inkling that her illness was this serious we can only speculate, but once again, she was being kept in ignorance of important factors affecting her life; even in this dire situation, she was being controlled and manipulated, people were choosing on her behalf what she needed to know and what she did not, rather than treating her like an adult. To be fair to William, he was in a tricky position. Ada's diagnosis came hot on the heels of her gambling disaster, which had not only left him severely out of pocket, but also left him very angry with his wife. He was furious that she had once again allowed herself to become so in debt that she needed bailing out, despite his stern warnings and her false promises.

But now all that seemed insignificant, as he was faced with the prospect that his wife was dying, so he did the only thing he felt he could, and that was to turn to Lady Byron for guidance. The time had finally come to confess to her the full extent of Ada's gambling but also, the seriousness of her illness. They had managed to keep the seriousness of the gambling a secret from her, but that could no longer be the case; the truth had to be laid out and the consequences had to be faced. You could be forgiven for thinking that the major piece of information that Lady Byron would be affected by was the tragic news that her daughter was dying, but that was not Lady Byron's style.

William travelled to see her at Leamington Spa. When he arrived, he handed her a letter which detailed the full medical explanation of Ada's illness and explained the gambling situation and the debts that had incurred. She was furious with William and blamed him for not taking greater care of Ada's moral wellbeing. She even went as far as accusing him of abandoning her to immorality. Upon hearing the news, Lady Byron's primary concern was Ada's morality and how that would impact her own reputation. She seemed to show little concern for her daughter's physical illness – the fact she was dying seemed to pass her by, it was the gambling that had upset and infuriated her the most. She could not believe that something had occurred to stain her morality and that seemed far more serious a concern than the fact her daughter was in the final stages of her life. The lies and deception meant that the relationship William had previously shared with his mother-in-law was now shattered. She could no longer trust him and wished she had known of all this earlier, as she could have stepped in. For, she thought, she was the only person who could have saved her daughter – she was not weak, like William.

Lady Byron made attempts to see Ada but she refused her requests, a decision that William supported his wife in. He was protecting her, for he knew that Ada would have probably suffered a verbal attack from her mother and seeing her would have been of no help; it would have made her already fragile state much worse. The relationship between mother and daughter had deteriorated since the trip to Newstead Abbey, and over time, Ada had learnt to become more and more dismissive of her mother and her attitudes. She no longer lived under her mother's influence, and this gave her the courage to turn her away from her home.

Sadly, this awakening came too late for Ada, as the cancer took control of her body. She was weakening fast and in incredible pain so, on 31 August 1851, the heart-breaking decision was made by William to finally tell his wife the full devastating details of her illness. By this time, she was fully addicted to laudanum and was haemorrhaging every few days. Ada battled the cancer bravely and she never lost her zest for life and continued with her scientific readings. Her brain remained strong, even if her ailing body did not. William admired his wife's strength and courage in the face of her illness and even harboured hopes that their relationship could be rebuilt in the last months they had together. Unfortunately, the ever-ruthless Lady Byron had other plans.

Rather than let her daughter rest and be peaceful, Lady Byron was determined to get the full story of Ada's gambling and all the other debts she had incurred. She was willing to settle her daughter's outstanding accounts but wanted a full itemised account of what was owed, so she employed her lawyer and lifelong friend Stephen Lushington to seek out the truth and get a full confession of all the money owed by Ada. He visited a frail-looking Ada in April 1852; the visit was successful and he manged to obtain a full account of her debts, including a list of who was owed what. He also learnt that Ada had pawned the Lovelace jewels in order to pay off John Crosse and to help pay off some of her debts. Luckily, Lady Byron managed to retrieve the jewels and promised Ada that she would keep this from William, but Crosse was devious and managed to gain access to Ada again and convinced her to tell him where they were being kept. She made the mistake of telling him and he promptly went out to pawn them again. Lady Byron once again managed to track them down but, on this occasion, she did not restore them to Ada; she kept them safe, away from the clutches of Crosse.

The relationship that Ada had with Crosse has never been fully understood. They may have conducted an affair, but then they may have just enjoyed a close friendship. It was this relationship that Lady Byron blamed for Ada's illness – she felt her daughter was being punished for her bad behaviour. Ever the hypochondriac, Lady Byron showed little sympathy towards Ada during her illness. Ada knew she would get very little sympathy from her mother, so initially she downplayed the seriousness of the illness. Once Lady Byron had discovered the full extent of Ada's money issues, she decided to step in and demand access to her daughter. Clearly, she was needed. William quite clearly had no idea what his wife was up to and had no control over her; he had reached a point at which he could no longer take care of Ada's finances and was pleased when Lady Byron stepped in.

Crosse was a sly man who had lived a double life as far as his relationship with Ada was concerned, and when Ada learnt that he was secretly married with children, she was devastated, duped yet again by a man who was only out for he could get from her. When Lady Byron learnt of all this, she took swift and decisive action by barring all of Ada's friends from seeing her. If anyone wanted access to Ada then they had to submit a request through her. Ada was allowed to receive correspondence and she expressed a wish to see her good friend Charles Dickens, so William wrote to him requesting he visit Ada. Dickens obliged and read passages to her from *Dombey and Son*, in particular the passages concerning the death of the young Paul Dombey. *Dombey and Son* was Ada's favourite novel and it must have brought her great comfort to have her dear friend by her side reading to her. Dickens described the meeting as sad, as he sat with his friend alone, and they talked of life and the future.

As time slowly dragged on, the illness got progressively worse. The pain grew to levels that Ada struggled to endure. On the days she felt strong enough, she would take a turn about the room but would so often be overcome and struck down by terrible pains that mattresses had to be placed in her rooms on the floors to prevent her from injuring herself, as she would often fall to the floor in agony. It was around this time, on one of her better days, that she sat for her portrait by Henry Phillip; his father Thomas had previously painted her father. He chose to depict Ada sitting at the piano. It is a difficult picture to look at, as you can clearly see from the image that Ada was in great pain. She appears very thin and seems tense, the pain etched on her face a far cry from the earlier paintings that show a lively, vivacious young woman.

On 15 August, Ada declared to William that she wished to be buried next to her father in the Byron vault at the church of St Mary Magdalene in the parish of Hucknall, near Newstead Abbey. Her request seems a strange one, considering she had never met her father and had no real links to the area. She had never lived at Newstead Abbey and had only visited once, but it was that visit the year before that must have prompted her to think of this as her preferred place of interment. She clearly felt it was right to be laid to rest as a Byron rather than a King or Milbanke.

Later that month, on 26 August, her youngest son Ralph returned home from Switzerland to visit his mother, but only a day later, the convulsions grew worse. By the 28th, Ada had begun having fits, and at 4.00 am on 29 August her pulse stopped for ten minutes and she slipped into a coma. By the 30th she had regained consciousness, but the level of pain had increased. That latest struggle prompted Ada to make the difficult decision to finally be honest with William, encouraged by Lady Byron. She wanted to talk about their marriage and about herself. She lovingly placed her arms around his neck and kissed him, then asked for his forgiveness, which he gave wholeheartedly, and then proceeded to make her confession.

We do not know exactly what she said to him – we can probably surmise it was about her supposed love affair with John Crosse and the pawned jewels – but whatever Ada said to her husband that day left him devastated. He was so heartbroken he turned away from his dying wife's bedside and walked out of the room, hid himself away and only returned to her bedside when her end was near. To his credit, William never spoke of what Ada confessed to him that day. We can look upon William's actions with scorn or pity. He had sacrificed a lot in the name of his wife's reputation, he had paid debts and dealt with the fact that she had had liaisons with other men, and also accepted that she had perhaps never truly loved him, but at the same time, Ada was on her death bed. The time had passed to be angry and resentful – there would have been no point in screaming and shouting, she had not the energy to fight, but abandoning her now left her vulnerable, in her mother's care.

Lady Byron seized on this opportunity and took full control over Ada once more, and she wasted no time in pressuring Ada to sign a document that confirmed her wickedness and lack of gratitude to her mother. It is doubtful that Ada would have been physically, or mentally, able to resist anything her mother put in front of her; in fact, it may have been a blessing in disguise that she was perhaps not fully aware of what she was signing. How sad it is to think a mother would do this to her dying daughter, thinking of herself and her reputation before the needs of her child.

Ada continued to linger on and by October, the children left her bedside. Her son Byron went to see his mother for the last time before leaving for Horsley Towers, where he picked up his newly acquired officer's uniform and then disappeared. He was finally tracked down in November in Liverpool, attempting to flee to America, but William insisted that he return to the navy he detested so much. Eventually he was posted to HMS *Victory* and later to Malta, before finally deserting. Ada was never told that her son had gone missing, so as not to cause her any undue stress and upset. After a short stay in America, he managed to return to England to a job in the shipyards of East London, riveting metal plates on the ships being built by Brunel. He died at a house in Wimbledon, close to where the current Centre Court stands, in his sister's arms, after collapsing on a boat. He was aged just 26 when he died, seemingly another victim to the Byron curse of dying young.

Ada clung to her mother as the end drew closer, but then she had no one else. William was present but owing to her recent confession, he remained just at her bedside. Having seen her children say goodbye and leave and her husband turn away from her, she had no one left but the mother who had spent her life manipulating and controlling her. It seemed inevitable that she should die in her company. We can only hope that when Ada actually needed her mother to be just that, she was able to step into that role and offer her dying daughter the comfort and support she needed. The time for games was over. Ada was dying, and the old arguments no longer mattered. She no longer needed to be controlled and coerced. For all the agony she had suffered over the last few months, the least Lady Byron could have done was to be there when her daughter needed her the most.

Ada King, Countess of Lovelace finally lost her long battle with cancer and slipped away on the evening of 27 November 1852, aged just 36, the same age her father was when he died. Her funeral was held a week later on 3 December. The *Nottinghamshire Guardian* reported that the funeral took place at midday and that 'Her remains are to be deposited in the same vault, and by the side of her father.' The coffin travelled from Great Cumberland Place, London to the George the Fourth Hotel, Nottingham on the Midland Railway. Here her body was to lay in state. On her coffin was laid her coronet and, just like her father before her, it was visited in great numbers by the public. The following morning, the body was taken from there via the old road to Hucknall Torkard. Mourners arrived by special train on the morning of the funeral, and these included the Earl of Lovelace, the current Lord Byron, the Hon. Locke King, Sir G. Crauford, Mr King, Dr Lushington, Col. Wildman, Woronzow Grieg, and Mr C. Noel. The cortege was met at the church by Rev. Curtis Jackson. He led the coffin down the aisle, where it was placed in front of the altar. On the coffin was a silver plate with the inscription:

> The Right Honourable Augusta Ada, wife of William,
>   Earl of Lovelace.
> And only daughter of George Gordon Byron.

Born December 10th, 1815
Died November 27th, 1852
Aged 37 years.

(Note that her age at the time of death is incorrect.)

Her plaque confirms her date of birth, her date of death, her marriage details, and the fact that she was the daughter of Lord Byron. There was no mention of her scientific achievements; why this is the case is unclear – it could indicate that her work was not considered to be of such importance at the time. It would only be much later that the full realisation of what she had uncovered would become prominent. Many of the congregation were moved by the solemn and silent service. Her velvet-covered coffin was carried down into the Byron vault, and there she was laid to rest next to her father. They may have been parted in life but they were finally reunited in death.

Despite the large crowds that lined the coffin's route, the funeral itself was a private affair attended only by close family and friends. Lady Byron did not attend her daughter's funeral. She had her reasons, and they probably included the fact that attending her husband's place of burial may have in some way indicated that she had forgiven him his sins; she seems unable to have looked past her own feelings to that of her daughter. There was also the ongoing dispute with William that may have kept her away. It is sad to think she did not attend her only child's funeral because of her issues with the men in Ada's life. Despite this, she did, however, build a large memorial in the grounds of Kirkby Mallory to preserve her daughter's memory.

The relationship between William and Lady Byron had broken down completely and they only communicated through her lawyer, Stephen Lushington. William had issues over the double pawning of the diamonds, but as Lady Byron had returned them to him, she could not see what his problem was. John Crosse never failed to miss an opportunity to make money and he quickly resorted to blackmail following Ada's death. He claimed to have over 100 letters from Ada, which could have damaged hers and William's reputation. In them, she declared her love for Crosse, but more worryingly, there was also a note signed by William consenting to his wife's gambling, proving he not only knew what she was doing but condoned her actions too. Maybe he did, but seeing as it was him who bailed Ada out, it seems of little consequence. Lady Byron wanted to refuse Crosse's demands but was finally convinced to pay him his demand of £600 for the incriminating letters. She had spent her life protecting Ada's reputation; it would have made little sense for her to let that be damaged following her death. Along with a £600 payout, Ada had also bequeathed Crosse a bloodstone signet ring and a lock of hair, both belonging to Lord Byron.

Lady Byron passed away peacefully at St George's Terrace from breast cancer on 16 May 1860 at the age of 67, and was laid to rest at Kensal Rise Cemetery. Before she died, Lady Byron told the full story of her tumultuous marriage to Harriet Beecher Stowe, who published the story nine years later. The task of trying to decipher the character of Lady Byron is a difficult one. On the face of it, she was a controlling, domineering woman who ruled her child's life with an iron fist. She saw it as her sole role in life to ensure Ada remained protected from her father until she reached an age in which she could face it. There is no denying that Lady Byron was a brave and courageous woman who saw that in order to save herself and her child, she had to turn her back on the man she loved, the man whose relationship defined her life. The early reputation of Lady Byron was not favourable; she was seen as cold, small minded, and was accused of poor judgement when it came to the separation. She is known as being the estranged wife of Lord Byron and the mother of Ada Lovelace, but she was much more than that. She was an intelligent woman who backed reform and was a staunch supporter of the movement that backed the abolition of slavery and of many other social causes. She was loved by her friends; they describe her as being shy, which was often mistaken for coldness, but affectionate and kind. It seems she was all these things to everyone except her own daughter.

William was advised not to attend his mother-in-law's funeral. Now that both Ada and young Byron Ockham had passed away, Ralph became her principal heir. He added the surnames Milbanke and Noel to his own and inherited the vast Wentworth estates, whilst his sister Anne inherited an annual allowance of £3,000, her grandmother's jewellery, ornaments and trinkets. William himself passed away on 29 December 1893, aged 88 years old. He remarried following Ada's death and had a further son with his second wife, Jane Jenkins.

Ada's life was cut tragically short by her illness, but nonetheless it was one of great success and achievement. Through her notes on the Analytical Engine, she managed to revolutionise the idea that machines could perform certain tasks that previously many only assumed could only have been done by humans. She could see beyond the current limitations of technology to a future in which machines could eliminate human error and advance human knowledge. Despite her clever mind, she lived a life of suppression and often suffered manipulation at the hands of those she ought to have been able to trust and, from the moment of her birth, she was destined to live a life less ordinary.

At the age of just four weeks old, her mother made a huge decision and carried her away from the family home and away from her father. Lady Byron felt the need to protect her daughter from the supposed threat of being too much like him in character and mind. He was notoriously dissolute and that was no environment to raise a child. Lady Byron's decision to bring Ada up under such a strict regime would have lasting effects on her and this suppression of her character, particularly in her younger years, caused her to have an unhappy and lonely upbringing. She was allowed no friends her own age to play with and those she did mix with were watched closely, just in case the games they played caused Ada too much excitement. Instead, she found herself mainly surrounded by adults, who watched her every move and reported back to Lady Byron anything that could have indicated immoral behaviour. Ada never enjoyed the carefree feeling that came with playing with friends – she never got to experience the joys of running about a garden on a summer's day. All of this she was deprived of simply because it could have caused her mind to become excitable and for her to have too much fun. Lady Byron may have thought she had her daughter's best interests at heart, but all she ended up achieving was the increased feeling of isolation her daughter felt. Whether that is what she hoped to achieve we cannot be sure, but there is often a sense that Lady Byron was punishing Ada for something. Maybe for being the daughter of Lord Byron, or maybe her looks reminded Lady Byron of her husband, or perhaps she had some mannerisms that resembled him. We do not know, but her heavy-handed parenting techniques left a lot to be desired.

Lady Byron was clearly besotted with her husband, and the fact the marriage failed in the manner it did must have been difficult for her to come to terms with. Every time she looked upon her daughter, she would have been reminded of this. Maybe she felt that if Ada had not been born, or if indeed if she had been a boy, her marriage to the wayward poet would have somehow survived, although Lord Byron's issues were so deep-rooted that it would have made no difference in the end whether the baby had been born a boy or a girl. The marriage was doomed from the start and nothing could have saved it. Having said all this, there is no suggestion that Ada was an unwanted child and I do believe Lady Byron loved her daughter in her own way; she perhaps did not go about showing this the right way. There is certainly strong evidence to suggest that Lady Byron wanted to remain attached to her husband in some way – even after his death, she continued to keep the link alive when she named their first grandson after him. With Lady Byron's link to her husband ending with his death, Ada was the direct connection to Lord Byron, and by choosing his name, she reaffirmed that connection even further; it kept the name of Byron and the legend he created alive and by doing so it kept him a part of Lady Byron's life.

Regardless of what Lady Byron's intentions were towards Ada during her childhood, as she got older, it would have been reasonable to assume she would relax her grip on Ada's life, but she was never willing to fully relinquish her control. As Ada reached adulthood, she still held her in a tight grip, watching every move and orchestrating every meeting. Marriage should have provided Ada with the opportunity to release herself from her mother's ever-watchful eye, but when she married William King, Lady Byron's need to control every aspect of her life eventually spread to her husband and their children. Soon all of their lives were under her scrutiny.

Appearances were always important to Lady Byron, and it was crucial that people believed everything she did was for the benefit of Ada. She was very good at giving the impression that she was doing her best for her poor child, appearing to sacrifice her own needs for her little girl, who was to be pitied. After all, with a father like that, she would need all the help she could get. Lady Byron was putting on a sacrificial show and enjoying the plaudits that came with it; she was the martyr and another victim of Lord Byron's cruel behaviour. Her reputation was that of being a good mother, a mother who had devoted her whole life to safeguarding her daughter, protecting her from rumour and scandal, always putting her first.

I would not for one moment suggest that Lady Byron was not a good mother to Ada; after all, we have not lived their lives, we do not know of every conversation, and surely there must have been some moments of tenderness between them, but her actions towards Ada on her deathbed do seem very callous and uncaring. Using an opportunity when you know the other person is incapable of reaction for your own gains seems like an unforgivable act, but for a mother to do that to her own child seems incomprehensible. It is a sad fact, but Lady Byron never quite seemed able to just be a mother to Ada. Rather than being supportive and understanding, she seemed to revel in Ada's misfortunes, constantly berating her if she trod down a wrong path. Rather than guiding her like a parent should, she seemed to punish Ada with more restrictions. Granted, she often cleared up the mess, but there was always a reason or motive for doing the things she did – it was almost as if she was scared to love her in a normal maternal way. That, of course, could just have been her nature rather than being deliberate.

Given the fractious relationship between mother and daughter, it would make for an interesting discussion to consider what kind of relationship Ada and Lord Byron would have had, had he lived longer. They might have been close as adults; it is difficult to accept that he would have continued to abstain from being a part of her life, especially when she married and had children of her own. Also, if Lord Byron had been fully aware of the suppression of his daughter and her mind, is it feasible to think he might possibly have stepped in and removed Ada from her mother's care? Whilst he agreed that Ada was not to be influenced by him or his work, the idea that her mind was being controlled to the extent it was might have rung alarms bells for him. He was adamant that he did not want Ada to follow him down the poetical path, but he would not have wanted her to have no thoughts or ideas of her own. How ironic it is to think that for all the suppression of her thoughts, Ada's mind would go on to be capable of such advanced thought. But again, her ability to have a mind that could process information in the way it did was down to Lady Byron's control over her education and the specific subjects she was taught. So, whilst we can bemoan and condemn the suppression of excitable thoughts, in essence, by doing that, she awoke and enabled a whole different part of Ada's brain that, albeit logical and methodical, did cause huge excitement for her and for others. Her brain was quite clearly very special and can be considered one of the greatest of her day.

The relationships in Ada's life were often complex. Her parental ones were irregular and her marriage with William followed a more friendly route than that of lovers. She had many liaisons with men that did not always leave her on the right side of a good reputation, and her children were often left out in the cold when it came to motherly love. We can learn a lot from Ada's death and the relationships she had with her family, what her life was like, and how she was treated by her loved ones. We can only speculate about what words she spoke to her husband days before she passed away, but I think we can safely assume that she was confessing to her illicit love affair with Crosse and maybe even the pawning of the Lovelace jewels; whatever it was, it hurt him enough to abandon her in her dying days. But was William's response an overreaction, a knee-jerk reaction to bad news? It does seem rather callous to turn away from your dying wife and resolve never to lay eyes on her again – what was he hoping to achieve by doing this? I find it difficult to conceive that William wanted to cause Ada extra pain on top of what she was already experiencing – he just does not seem the kind of man who would do this. It was very out of character, therefore we can only surmise that William was hurt very deeply by Ada's news. He had supported her throughout their marriage and it must have felt like a huge blow to him, like she had betrayed him in more ways than one. We know the marriage may not have been one of passion, it may not have set Ada's world alight, and William may have realised that he had married above his station. He was an admirer of Lord Byron and seized the opportunity to marry his daughter, but maybe he had taken on more than he realised, and maybe Lady Byron's help was not to be sniffed at after all. Regardless of the circumstances behind the marriage, it turned out to be a union of respect on both sides; we know this as William made sure Ada's wish to be buried at Hucknall was carried out. Lady Byron would not have been pleased to discover her daughter's request, but William insisted.

Ada's relationship with her children had always been strained, in a different way to her own relationship with her mother. She was often distant and, by her own confession, she was never a doting mother and struggled to form a strong bond with any of her children. One reason as to why she may have struggled was that she had no experience of what that bond should be like. Lady Byron rarely showed her affection in the way a mother ought to, so Ada had no firm foundation on which to base her own skills as a parent. William would have struggled with this too, given his fraught relationship with his own mother. Unfortunately, he carried this through to his own dealings with his children, and they never enjoyed a close relationship. But each of the Lovelace children felt the loss of their mother keenly. The young Byron, Lord Ockham, left to return to sea before his mother had passed and from what we know, Anne and Ralph both spent time with their mother in her final weeks, but as her drawn-out death dragged on, their presence became less and less.

But as it had been throughout her life, it was her mother who dominated Ada's life when the end came. She stepped in and took full control of the sick room, which, to be fair, was probably a good move, what with William brooding elsewhere. Ada's mother seized the reins. Unfortunately, Lady Byron saw this as an opportunity to finally have her daughter back under her control. Since the Newstead Abbey visit and the gambling incidents, she had stepped back from her daughter's life, which had left Ada with a feeling that she had finally broken free from her mother's grasp, but with no William around to use as a buffer, Lady Byron now had free rein to resume her dominance and control the comings and goings to the inner sanctum of Ada's death chamber. She made sure she vetted every visitor before allowing them through, and not many, if any, made it.

Were these the actions of a concerned mother? Possibly. Knowing that her only child was dying a slow, painful death, you can forgive her for trying to protect Ada's dignity at the most vulnerable time of her life. Or was this the Lady Byron of old, wanting to control every aspect of her life? The forcing of Ada to sign the documents that exonerated her from any of Ada's misdemeanours is not the action of a loving, concerned mother; it is more the action of someone who is concerned over nothing but preserving and vindicating her own actions. We can only imagine how Lady Byron felt when she discovered that Ada's final wishes were to be buried in Nottinghamshire next to her errant father, but her refusal to attend the funeral speaks volumes. After all the time that had passed, Lady Byron could still not look beyond her own feelings. Lady Byron is often described as being cold-hearted and incapable of giving her daughter the maternal care she needed. When all was said and done, all she was able to offer her was an intellectual relationship instead.

As we look back over Ada's life, it is clear to see she was a conflicted person, one capable of greatness and yet, on the other hand, one who suffered periods of deep depression and anxiety. She suffered an oppressive childhood at the hands of a mother who never let her be a child, one who constantly had her under supervision, and one who would deal with any naughty behaviour with a stern hand. From childhood, she moved to marriage and, whilst William does not come across as a strict husband, paying Ada a meagre allowance of £300 meant he could control her spending; he probably did this on the advice of Lady Byron. The constraints of marriage and motherhood supressed Ada further. So much was kept from her regarding her father, which was understandable from Lady Byron's point of view, but did this constant suppression just cause Ada to want to rebel further? Are we to believe that she never sneaked a peep of her father's portrait behind the green velvet curtain? I think not, she had an intelligent and inquisitive mind, so I think we can safely presume she did. There were definitely two sides to the life of Ada Lovelace: Ada the passionate, often conflicted, wife, mother, and daughter, and on the other, Ada the mathematician, who, by the translation of and addition to notes, showed what computers could achieve. Her understanding was far beyond her time, and it is that Ada that we celebrate today.

Chapter Seven

The Byron Curse

It has been a long-held belief that the Byron family were under some kind of curse, that bad blood had flowed through the veins of a family that so often courted scandal and outrage. Their most famous member, the romantic poet Lord Byron, was the rockstar of his age, a literary superstar the like of which, before him, the country had never known. He had the kind of star quality that we see in today's big-name celebrities, with the ability to command any room he walked into. It was not just his words on the page that brought him attention – his physical appearance was also widely talked about. He was described as an Adonis, with thick wavy dark hair and a strong jaw, a feature Ada inherited, his skin was pale, and his mouth as red as a cherry, with an aquiline nose. He was famed for his beautiful looks; they were one of his most distinguishing features, along with the billowing white shirt and long black coat that he wore. Often he had women, and men, hanging off his every word. His demeanour was flawed; he could be happy one minute and, in the next breath, he was plunged into the deepest of depressions, haunted by his heinous sins, the two most serious of which were sodomy and incest. Once his marriage to Lady Byron had broken down, he was on borrowed time. Rumours were now circulating regarding his private life, and as sodomy was illegal at that time, he could have faced imprisonment or death, or at the very least ruination.

Byron's life in England was over. He had been the darling of the press – they had built him up to hero status, but now they stood ready to destroy him. They called him wicked and depraved, and exile was the only option left to him. As he sailed out of Dover, he left debts of up to £30,000, which puts Ada's gambling debts into perspective. He headed first for France and from there he travelled through Belgium to Geneva and then on to Venice, where he settled, before moving onto Greece. Throughout his travels, he had a string of lovers; he even fathered a further daughter on a young lady named Claire Clairmont, the stepsister of Byron's friend Mary Shelley, author of *Frankenstein*. Their daughter Allegra was born in 1817, and after an initial unsettled start to her life, baby Allegra was taken into the custody of her father, on the condition that she had little or no contact with her mother. He also requested that her surname be altered from Byron to Biron. He did not wish people to think that Allegra and Ada were related – they were not to be considered in the same way. She was a difficult child and often wreaked havoc in Byron's household. She seemed to have inherited the Byron gene for wild behaviour and, soon enough, she was sent to live in a convent by her father. He felt she would benefit from a stricter upbringing in a better climate.

The young Allegra sadly passed away in Italy at just 5 years old. It is said that Byron was left devastated by his young daughter's death; he felt guilty that he had not provided her with a better upbringing and felt himself responsible for her life of neglect. Whether Ada knew about her younger half-sister we do not know; given that she had no real knowledge of Medora, it is unlikely that she would have been told any news regarding Allegra's existence. It is interesting to consider that Byron took custody of Allegra while he never exerted this right over Ada; being left at home in England was perhaps a blessing in disguise.

Life on the continent continued to move at fast pace for Lord Byron, who claimed to have bedded over 200 women during this short time. This is the image of Lord Byron that stands the test of time – this is what we know and recognise as Lord Byron, the greatest poet of his age but also one with the greatest and most debauched of characters. He was the epitome of the gothic hero, the dark coat and billowing white shirt, which he always wore open at the neck. It is this image that people think of when they think of Lord Byron, a beautiful, tormented, romantic soul.

But what of Ada, his only legitimate child. Did she inherit any of the so-called Byron curse? Did the Byron curse even exist? Did the bad blood run down from the 'Wicked Lord'? Was Lady Byron right to try to shield her from all this? Well, she certainly thought it was real, and she had the doctor's tests to prove it. Lord Byron was disturbed in the mind, and she worked hard to make sure her daughter was not tainted by it. If she did display any of the characteristics, then they were quickly nipped in the bud. If by chance any scandal seeped through, measures were put in place to prevent them catching on.

Ada was protected in a way that her father never was. If Lord Byron had had someone like this when he was growing up, then perhaps he might have turned out differently, but his mother, who was badly used by her husband, spent much of her time in a depressive state, so it is little wonder her only child suffered too. Lord Byron's relationship with his mother was a complex one to say the least. She probably tried her best, but with little money, she struggled to raise him in comfort. Byron was born with a deformity to his foot, which caused him to limp his whole life. His mother employed numerous doctors to try to cure him of this, but many of the treatments caused him severe pain and discomfort. It was described as being a 'club foot', which also caused him to suffer muscle wastage in his lower leg. Special boots were made that had padded sides to hide this leanness of his calf and a built-up sole which helped to disguise the condition. Byron always wore long-length trousers and any paintings of him often covered the afflicted leg up. The pain and suffering caused by his leg raised his anger towards his mother; he blamed her for it and she often taunted him. The deformity tormented him his whole life. He had no memories of his father at all – he deserted his family when Byron was only young, but he worshipped him regardless of this. In his mind, his father was a hero. All this is starting to sound very familiar; complex relationships with your mother and an absent father seems to be a prerequisite of being a Byron.

Lady Byron could not expect to control every aspect of Ada's life, although she tried her best to. She might have been able to have her spied on as a child, but as she grew older and wiser to her mother's motives, it became harder for her to monitor what was going on. If Ada was deemed to be suffering from the so-called curse, then no matter how much Lady Byron tried to intercede, it would come through. Victorian society thought bad blood was inherited through nature, and no amount of nurture could cure it. If we look at Ada's life as a whole, then there are some definite markers that would ring alarm bells to indicate she had been tainted with the curse.

Firstly, we have the attempted elopement with her tutor. On the face of it, this may have simply been a schoolgirl fantasy – she may well have believed herself to be in love with an older man and let herself get swept away in the romance of it all. Or it may have been an open rebellion against the strict upbringing that Lady Byron had enforced on her. Either way, it was a reckless act on her part, and she must have known full well that it was wrong and there would be serious repercussions when they were discovered. Whether Ada would have gone through with the marriage or not we will never know. This could just have been a cry for attention on her part – being so desperate to bring about a change in her life that she felt she had no choice, she seized the moment and went for it. It was a huge lapse in judgement on her part; her heart was definitely being ruled by her head, a very Byronic trait, and the fact she went as far as running away from the family home would indicate she had a wild streak in her, but could that streak be tamed? Lady Byron would have been fuming when she discovered what Ada had done and must also have panicked, hoping that all her hard work had not been in vain.

It was hoped that Ada's marriage to William would provide her with some stability, which it did to a certain degree. It was certainly a lot more successful than that of her parents – at least the Lovelaces managed to stay together and provide their children with some sort of family unit; it was far from perfect, but it resembled something normal. As we have already discussed, Ada was not madly in love with William. It is as though she married him because she felt she had no option. She had to marry someone, and he seemed a reasonable man who could provide her with every comfort she needed. Again, this resonates strongly with her parents' marriage. We know Byron dreaded his wedding day and he approached it like a man on his way to the gallows; his fate was sealed so he might as well just get on with it and accept his doom. I don't think we can say Ada felt the same way about marrying William – we do know there was love and respect there – but that did not prevent her having extramarital liaisons, and she never seemed totally happy with William. Maybe she settled, just like her father had.

But there was much to be grateful for in her marriage. Her father was prone to violent rages – he would smash furniture to pieces and would rage angrily at Lady Byron, and she would have no option but to sit there and take it. He often tormented and ridiculed her, especially if Augusta was in residence at the time, but William was solid and dependable, which was just what Ada needed, and there was never any indication that he had been violent towards his wife. She often questioned her suitability as a wife and mother, and Lord Byron similarly doubted himself, but whilst he chose to remove himself from the domestic sphere, Ada did not. Her mind suffered for it, as she felt stunted, but she would never have wanted to cause William any public shame. She respected him too much for that. Marriage is a difficult subject as far as Ada is concerned. She wavered from being happily married to regretting it; if she had married someone else, then maybe she would have been happier, but Ada would never have been given free rein to marry who she wished, just in case they took advantage of her fragile emotions, so William was the best choice for her. He provided her with a cover for most of their married life, just in the same way Lady Byron did for her husband, although Ada's sins were much less serious.

One major incident that dominated Ada's life was her addiction to gambling on the horses, a pursuit enjoyed by some of her forefathers too, and it was all undertaken for the sake of earning more money. The 'Wicked Lord' Byron bet on the horses in a bid to ease his depleted Newstead Abbey estate, whilst Ada did it to help build the Analytical Machine. So then, is it fair to tarnish her with the same brush? Did she really have an addiction, or did she just see an opportunity to make some money, fast? If we are to believe that Ada wanted to raise the funds to help Babbage then her intentions were good and honourable, and she had a fixed aim in her mind. Surely we could only call her an addict if she continued to gamble after she had achieved her aim. Sadly, we will never know – the losses were so great that there was no way she could have continued even if her health had allowed her to.

In theory, Ada had a good idea, but she perhaps did not approach it in the right manner. She should have had the sense to understand that no mathematical equation could help win on the horses. Surely she must have understood that there were external forces she could have no control over; she would have been better off just studying the form and taking a chance. Maybe it was not the money that drew her to the races, maybe it was the excitement, the thrill of the chase, a moment to abandon all propriety and to let herself be immersed in something fun. She had perhaps finally found something in her life that she enjoyed, something that she knew her mother would never allow herself to get involved with as it went against her moral code. Finally, Ada could get a thrill from something away from her mother's gaze – if she happened to win some money along the way, all the better, but perhaps it was down to the sheer joy it brought her.

Whatever her reasons were for gambling, she lost big. Her calculations proved wrong, which must have hurt; she truly believed she could come up with a formula because if anyone could have, she could. The disaster of the gambling threated to derail all the good work she had done with the Analytical Engine; she was lucky that it did not cloud people's judgement of her work. Gambling was certainly a vice, and not one a lady of Ada's status should have been involved in, so it was imperative that her losses and involvement in the scheme were covered up. Ada was extremely fortunate to have someone on hand like William to help conceal her indiscretions.

The addictions did not end on the racecourse, though. Both Ada and her father were addicted to laudanum and suffered with eating disorders in their lives. Lord Byron would often starve himself in a bid to remain trim but would then gorge on food to the point he got stuck in a vicious cycle. For Ada, her obsession with food came after the birth of her children, when she may have carried a little more weight than before. This obsessive personality they both seem to have ruled over their lives at different times; both seemed to home in on one area, and it became an all-consuming need to sate that appetite. Laudanum was used to offer them an escape – whether that was from pain due to illness or just a desire to relieve depression, both took it without concerns and in vast quantities.

One final aspect of the supposed Byron curse was an early death. Ada suffered terribly with her health throughout her life and lost that battle at the age of 36, just like her father had. They had both suffered tragically sad ends, their geniuses dying far too soon, their brains being far superior to their physical selves. One can only imagine what great things either may have gone on to achieve had they lived longer. Lord Byron could have produced another epic poem to sit alongside *Childe Harold's Pilgrimage* and *Don Juan*, and Ada could have progressed to see further advancements of computer science. She might even have had the will and desire to get the Analytical Engine built. Florence Nightingale made a poignant comment regarding Ada's long, drawn-out illness. She felt her mind was to great and powerful and would simply not die – it was too strong for her body. What a thought that is, that Ada was so intelligent that her mind outlived her physical self.

The early death and the contrasting emotions about love make Ada a romantic heroine. She was an intelligent woman who was unable to fulfil her truest potential, she suffered great pains with her health, and her mind was at times fractured, leading to bouts of depression. She seemed to torture herself over her suitability as a daughter, wife, and mother, when in fact if she had just been allowed to live without restriction or censor, she could have thrived more than she did. But did she suffer from the curse? Did that curse even exist? Who really knows? She certainly had some tendencies towards recklessness and the argument over nature and nurture is an interesting one, but can it be called a curse or is it simply bad luck? Genetics certainly played a part in Ada's life and, to be fair, in her father's as well – both had forefathers that went before them with questionable traits.

Lady Byron's censure certainly kept Ada on the right path. If she had been left to run wild then maybe she would have gone down paths she should not have and that could have ruined her completely. If she had been successful on her first bid for freedom with her tutor, then it is highly unlikely she would have furthered her studies and achieved what she did, so we do have Lady Byron to thank for that. But at the end of the day, Ada had Byron blood. Whether that was tainted or not is irrelevant, as she was always going to resemble him in some way or other and there was nothing anyone could have done to change that. She certainly inherited his genius – it was just applied in different manner. He had a way with words and she with numbers, but both equally excelled in their fields. I like to come back to the thought of how the two would have got on as adults. Had Ada been able to meet Byron the man, she would have been able to make her own judgements, on him but likewise, what would he have made of his daughter's achievements? No doubt he would have been proud, but the world Ada inhabited had moved on so much in the time since her father's death, and sadly we will never know. But what a remarkable thought it is to think of them together as adults, discussing all things scientifically poetical.

Chapter Eight

Ada's Legacy

'That brain of mine is something more than merely mortal; as time will show.'

The above quote for me epitomises Ada and her work completely, but just how good was she at mathematics? Her biographer Dorothy Stein described her as only having a rudimentary understanding of maths and claimed she struggled with certain algebraic equations, so, it would appear not as good as we imagine, but it was her level of understanding that sets her apart. She had a fervent imagination, and it was this that when combined with her mathematical knowledge resulted in the notes and the Analytical Engine.

Ada King, Countess of Lovelace was a unique woman who achieved a level of greatness that those of her age could only dream of. She outshone many men in her field and achieved something that most women could not even conceive of. Learning and understanding what she did during her work with the Analytical Engine means that her name has become synonymous with the computer science of our age.

It was during the Second World War that Alan Turing, another great mathematician who was not fully appreciated due to social stigmas, stumbled across her workings in the now famous *Note G*. He was trying to create a machine that would be able to crack the German codes and in turn prevent large-scale bombing and loss of life. He explored the same ideas that Ada had done 100 years earlier, though, she felt, 'The Analytical Engine has no pretensions to originate anything. It can do whatever we know how to order it to perform. Only when computers originate things should they be believed to have minds.' Turing called this *Lady Lovelace's Objection*. It was his idea that any universal computer should have the capability of human thought – what we would now call artificial intelligence (AI) and how the modern-day computer works. He believed that any computer could replace human thought, providing it had the appropriate machinery and computer codes to do so. It is easy to pass judgement on Ada's ideas and say she was wrong, but we must take into consideration the fact that she wrote 100 years earlier and could not have possibly imagined how far computer science could go. She could not have been able to envisage the computers we use today, although she was incredibly advanced for her era and what she worked on with Babbage was exceptional for the day. It was Turing's discovery of the long-forgotten *Note G* that brought Ada and her work back into the public's consciousness, and over time, she began to be recognised for the role she played in creating the first computer algorithm.

Unsurprisingly, there are many people today, mainly men, it has to be said, who claim Ada could not possibly have been responsible for the notes in the Menabrea Translations and that she must have had the help of a man, namely Babbage, who assisted her. The suggestion is that she simply copied from Babbage's own notes and claimed them for her own, as there was no way she could have understood what the Analytical Engine was capable of or known the mathematical equations used. This is a preposterous idea. It is not to say she had no help or guidance – it was complex work. I am sure there were many occasions on which she and Babbage discussed her findings, altered certain things, and adjusted figures, so yes, she may have been guided to a certain degree by others, but *Note G* is the work of Ada Lovelace and Ada Lovelace only. Babbage was one of the most eminent scientists of the day and a proud man too, so the idea that he would be happy for her to take the credit for his own work does seem to be slightly far-fetched. We know that he was keen to be recognised for his work, so he would simply not allow this. As for Ada herself, she does not come across as a woman who would take credit for someone else's work; she was principled and dignified and would not seek to reap rewards from the endeavours of others.

Whether it is the fact that Ada was a woman that has caused so many to question her ability we can only speculate, and this is a point we can argue all day long, but it cannot be denied that Ada had a fundamental understanding of mathematics and was more than capable of working out and suggesting what capabilities a machine like the Analytical Engine could have. It simply does not make sense to say she did this if she did not, as it benefits no one. Babbage was passionate about his engine and would not have wanted any doubt to linger over its capabilities. But we cannot dismiss her work based on her gender. She was Lord Byron's daughter who liked to gamble and take laudanum, but these factors do not make her incapable of such reasoned thought and certainly do not give people the right to dismiss her and her work. What is fair to say is that Ada was a trailblazer; she was a woman who was never going to be put neatly into one box and be one thing or another, and because of her achievement, she is now someone that women today can look to for inspiration.

The voice we hear most today is that of support and acknowledgement for her work, and her role within the STEM (Science, Technology, Engineering, and Maths) community cannot be underestimated. She has become a focus for women all over the world; she shows them that they can achieve great things within these disciplines, they should no longer be male-dominated areas, they should be open to anyone who has the interest and capability to perform well in them, regardless of age, colour, or gender.

In a bid to encourage more girls to study in these fields, Ada's achievements are taught to young children in England and Wales as part of the Key Stage 3 curriculum educational rollout. The focus is aimed mainly at girls in the hope that it will encourage them to pursue careers in the STEM industries, an area that has previously seen a low intake of female students but is now thankfully on the rise. There are also plenty of books about her achievements aimed at children of school age. The *Little People, Big Dreams* series documents the lives of many women who are celebrated for their achievements, and I was surprised to be able to collect a number of these from my local library, proving that there is a demand for information about Ada and her life.

One of the biggest accolades that has been bestowed on Ada is the fact she has her very own appreciation day; the second Tuesday of October is known worldwide as Ada Lovelace Day. The first was designated in 2009 by technologist Suw Charman-Anderson and is used to celebrate the roles and achievements of women in STEM. This cements Ada's place amongst the ranks of influential women that today's young girls who want to consider a role within the STEM subjects see as their role models. A few years ago, female school leavers may have been discouraged from pursuing these kinds of subjects, thinking of them as being accessible to male only applicants; girls were sometimes told they were not clever enough to study such scientific subjects and they should concentrate more on the female-orientated careers such as nursing and clerical roles. But raising the profile of women like Ada means these girls have someone they can aspire to be like. She is rightly held up alongside women such as Amelia Earhart and Marie Curie as an example of what women can achieve in the so-called male-dominated subjects.

Taking into consideration Ada's fantastic achievements and knowing that she now forms part of the national curriculum, I became interested in knowing if she had managed to eclipse her father in terms of recognition, so I decided to hold a poll on Twitter for school-aged children. I was expecting Lord Byron to come out on top, but surprisingly more were aware of Ada's work and achievements than they were of his poetry. The emergence of a more female-focused curriculum is evident; more books are being written specifically with young girls in mind about inspiring women. The shift in focus is clear – it is now becoming an important strategy to teach and show girls they can achieve whatever they desire, and it is remarkable that Ada is one of the figures used to inspire them.

The image of Ada is perhaps not known as widely as her father's, but during her lifetime, she sat for many portraits. The most famous of these was painted in 1840 by Alfred Edward Chalon. It is a watercolour picture that shows Ada as a young, pretty, vivacious woman. She is looking over her shoulder, dressed in a lilac gown, holding what appears to be a fan in her hands. It is this picture that is emblazoned across posters, T-shirts and other memorabilia and is the lasting image that that we associate with Ada Lovelace. She looks far from being a mathematical genius, but it is the image that prevails.

Other well-known images include miniatures of Ada as a child, a daguerreotype taken by Antoine Claudet, and the haunting image of Ada at the piano, months before her death. Along with the Chalon painting, the other well-known lasting image of Ada is a full-length oil on canvas portrait by Margaret Carpenter, which was painted in 1836, the same year that she gave birth to her first child. Ada is depicted in a long white dress with a red cape draped over her shoulders. It is an altogether different kind of image than the later Chalon picture. Carpenter captures a much more wholesome ladylike view of Ada, whereas the Chalon image shows Ada in a more playful mood. Ada was not a fan of the Carpenter painting and claimed that, 'I conclude she is bent on displaying the whole expanse of my capacious jaw bone, upon which I think the word mathematics should be written.' The painting was purchased by the government in 1953 for the Ministry of Works, whilst the Chalon painting forms part of the Science Museum's collection.

Given all that Ada achieved in her life, can we say that she broke free from her father's shadow? Yes, I feel we can comfortably say she did, as she achieved something that was so far ahead of her time. Lord Byron reaches into our world with his poetic words – we study them and break them down to understand their meaning, but we can never go back to that moment in time and fully understand the person. Ada was able to reach into the future and touch our world in a more tangible way; we can relate her work to our own computers, the laptops we sit at that perform the tasks she envisaged, making her a much more relatable figure. She is so revered in the scientific world that she appeared as a character in an episode of the BBC's *Doctor Who* in 2020 when she joined the Doctor and Babbage in saving the universe. In fact, Ada has appeared in various films, books, plays, and TV series. Her persona is often used to characterise someone who is clever and able to think logical matters through, and she is spirited and relatable. In fact, in 1980, the Department of Defense in the USA honoured Ada by naming their computer language after her. Now her name is also being attached to modern-day graphics and gaming applications, which shows her legacy still continues to thrive. She has become a cult hero.

She is rightly and justly recognised as someone who revolutionised thought, someone who had the foresight to believe in her abilities and her knowledge and to be brave enough to put that down on paper to be scrutinised by the world – the male-dominated world at that. It is fascinating to think of what Lord Byron would have made of his daughter's work, how he would have adjusted to having a daughter who was a genius. She may have excelled in her field, just as he had in his, but those fields were very different when all is said and done. We are aware of the supposed curse of the Byron madness, the immorality, and the debauchery, but what of the Byron genius? There can be no doubt that Ada inherited that, although we must not overlook the role Lady Byron played when it comes to discussing Ada's intelligence, as she herself was incredibly well-taught in the logical subjects and excelled in her own right.

Ada has also become a steampunk hero; in ideas that hark back to her childhood and her plans for a steam-powered flying machine, she has become an icon of all things advanced that could be powered by steam. Ada fits so perfectly into this genre. Steampunk is a branch of science fiction that is based in the past, usually the Victorian age, and inspires machinery that is powered by steam. The costumes are often described as quirky and with a twist. One cannot help but wonder what inventions Ada might have come up with had she lived in an age of electricity and more modern manufacturing. We could all have been using electrified flying machines rather than cars. Her take on modern technology would have been fascinating. Her ingenuity means it is right and proper that Ada takes her place alongside the greatest inventors, scientists, and mathematicians that have ever lived.

Her life was recognised by English Heritage in 1992 when they erected a Blue Plaque at the home she shared with William at St James's Square, London. It states simply:

Ada Countess of Lovelace
1815–1852
Pioneer of Computing lived here

Later, in 2017, Hinckley and Bosworth Borough Council also dedicated a Blue Plaque in Ada's memory at Kirkby Mallory. The inscription reads:

Ada Lovelace
(1815–1852)
pioneering mathematician and programmer
Daughter of famed poet Lord Byron,
Kirkby Hall was her childhood home

Touchingly, this plaque was unveiled at a special ceremony on 10 October, Ada Lovelace Day. Following her daughter's early death, Lady Byron arranged for a memorial to be built in the churchyard of Kirkby Mallory; it remains as a permanent reminder of the greatness Ada achieved in her short life.

Although her work was never fully appreciated during her lifetime, her name has remained important and influential in the work later done in understanding the role of computers and their capabilities. Her understanding of computer science earnt her the moniker the

'Enchantress of Numbers', and she is now considered an ideal role model for young women who are looking at a career in the once male-dominated areas of STEM. Some may argue that given her aristocratic background, the rumours of extramarital affairs, and massive gambling debts she should not be considered a positive influence on young women, but Ada deserves to be applauded based solely on her scientific achievements. Her private life was only part of her persona and none of that takes away from her brilliant mind and abilities. It is very difficult to cover all the various ways in which Ada has been remembered and recognised. Her influence and name are now so far-reaching that she touches many areas of STEM and she rightly deserves all the recognition she has received.

The name Byron did not contribute to Ada's success, it simply came down to her incredible brain, and for that she is rightly considered one of the most influential women in history, whose story deserves to be told.

Bibliography

Bond, G. & Kenyon Jones, C., *Dangerous to Show: Byron and His Portraits* (Unicorn, London, 2020)

Brand, E., *The Fall of the House of Byron* (John Murray, London, 2021)

Cooper, T., *National Portrait Gallery: A Portrait of Great Britain* (National Portrait Gallery Publications, 2014)

Essinger, J., *Ada's Algorithm: How Lord Byron's Daughter Launched the Digital Age Through the Poetry of Numbers* (Gibson Square, London, 2018)

Dennison, M., *Queen Victoria: A Life of Contradictions* (St. Martin's Press, London, 2014)

Doherty, A., *Ada Lovelace: The Fantastically Feminist (and Totally True) Story of the Mathematician Extraordinaire* (Wren & Rook, London, 2019)

Gray, J., *I, Ada: Rebel. Genius. Visionary* (Anderson Press, London, 2020)

Hollings, C., Martin, U., & Rice, A., *Ada Lovelace: The Making of a Computer Scientist* (The Bodleian Library, Oxford, 2018)

Hughes, K., *Victorians Undone: Tales of the Flesh in the Age of Decorum* (Fourth Estate, London, 2017)

Lansdown, R., *Byron's Letters and Journals* (Oxford University Press, Oxford, 2017)

Larman, A., *Byron's Women* (Head of Zeus, London, 2016)

MacCarthy, F., *Byron: Life and Legend* (Faber & Faber, London, 2003)

McGann, J. J., *Lord Byron: The Major Works* (Oxford University Press, Oxford, 2008)

O'Brien, E., *Byron in Love* (Weidenfeld & Nicolson, London, 2009)

Padua, S., *The Thrilling Adventures of Lovelace and Babbage: The (Mostly) True Story of the First Computer* (Penguin, London, 2016)

Peattie, A., *The Private Life of Lord Byron* (Unbound, London, 2019)

Peal, R., *Meet the Georgians* (William Collins, London, 2021)

Seymour, M., *In Byron's Wake* (Simon & Schuster, London, 2019)

Vegara, I. S. & Yamamoto, Z., *Ada Lovelace: Little People, Big Dreams* (Lincoln Children's Books, London, 2018)

Woolley, B., *The Bride of Science: Romance, Reason and Byron's Daughter* (Pan Books, London, 2015)

Online Resources

The Bodleian Library: www.bodleian.ox.ac.uk

The Encyclopaedia Britannica: www.britannica.com

The British Newspaper Archive: www.britishnewspaperarchive.co.uk

The British Library: www.bl.uk

The Computer History Museum: www.computerhistory.org

The Government Art Collection: www.artcollection.gov.uk

Newstead Abbey: www.newsteadabbey.org.uk

St Mary Magdalene Church, Hucknall: www.hucknallparishchurch. org.uk

The Science Museum: www.sciencemuseum.org.uk

Index